What God Says to Good Men in Bad Marriages

Gordon Simmons

Published by Gordon Simmons, 2024.

While every precaution has been taken in the preparation of this book, the publisher assumes no responsibility for errors or omissions, or for damages resulting from the use of the information contained herein.

WHAT GOD SAYS TO GOOD MEN IN BAD MARRIAGES

First edition. January 5, 2024.

Copyright © 2024 Gordon Simmons.

Written by Gordon Simmons.

What God Says to Good Men in Bad Marriages

By:

Rev. Gordon Simmons Th.M.

INTRODUCTION

It's so sad to say but in my marriage the juice has not been worth the squeeze, please help me God!

I'm tired of being blamed for everything. Ever notice at church service every Mother's Day how women are glorified but on every Father's Day men are demonized? The last Father's Day service I attended the Pastor preached a sermon the women loved. Its premise was 'no matter how bad your wife acted you were to honor and praise her'. An interesting topic to preach on the day fathers are to be honored. The assumption being that wives are good, pure, and self-sacrificing but the husbands are disserting, undisciplined, egocentric, and basically should work on being better husbands by accepting the sub-par performance of their spouses. I wanted to scream 'If I had a better wife I would have been a better husband'. I grieve with men who are left unfulfilled in their marriages. God designed marriage to be a blessing but if all you have experienced is a burden then this work speaks to what God has to say to you.

> It's so sad to say but in my marriage the juice has not been worth the squeeze.

As a man if you are married in a modern, western, feminist society then you are tired of being blamed for everything that goes wrong in your marriage. I counsel men to be prepared to accept that in a woman's mind everything that goes wrong will be his fault but everything that goes right will be because of her holiness and goodness. Hasn't that been the experience of your dysfunctional marriage? No need in being upset with your spouse because she doesn't seem capable of admitting any fault in herself. You are God's designated leader of your family and therefore responsible for dealing with all of her imperfections. Don't become like Adam and place the blame on God for giving you this woman, you chose her and probably for all the wrong reasons. She has become your burden to bear.

Women have a way in any situation of becoming the victim and placing the fault on you. If she spends the bill money on shoes the fault doesn't lay in her mismanaging of the family budget but in your not making enough money to support your family. If she wrecks the family car it will not be because she was reading a text on her mobile but because you have given her too many things to do. If you are unfaithful it is because all men are dogs but if she is unfaithful it is because you have not met her emotional needs. If you insist, as the leader of your family, on focusing on one of her faults that is causing the demise of your marriage she will retort 'yea, but what about you?' again shifting the blame off her and onto you. No one likes to admit to fault but if fault is going to be dealt with then it has to be admitted too. Many men tell me that their wives will never admit they are wrong, and honestly I see this more than the gender inverse in couples counseling. Many women struggle with admitting they are wrong, and instead of this being a narcissistic issue (although certainly sometimes it is), it really stems from massive insecurity and low self-esteem.

It is in the nature of a man to protect his wife and live in cooperation with her but lately in our western culture men having to bear all the burden of fault in a marriage makes the juice not worth the squeeze. Unless we can talk honestly about where half of the problems of marriage come from then we will only have half marriages. I know that in our society this honest discussion only encompasses the half of the problems that men cause. In this society it is taboo to consider that a problem may reside in the woman. Have you ever read in any Christian publication on marriage that deals with the wife having an issue? Well, if you haven't this one does and that of necessity because unless all the problems of modern marriage are dealt with men will continue to drop out of marriage. If half of the problems of a troubled marriage originate in the woman yet women can't admit to having innate problems then what hope is there for men to ever experience the joy of marriage God intended? Many men who are experiencing difficulties in their marriage is because your spouse is exhibiting some of the symptoms of Narcissistic Personality Disorder (NPD), not that she has full blown (NPD) but some of its symptoms. While people with narcissistic personality disorder can be superficially charming and likable at first, this false persona wears off quickly. Narcissists tend to be hypersensitive to criticism and highly defensive when they're offended, which is often how their difficult personalities are revealed to others. When offended, someone with NPD will often become highly defensive, reactive, and even aggressive or hostile. Never being able to admit fault needs to be addressed via therapy. Many of our marriages are messed up because we were so blind to what we married and unprepared to address the issues that women infected by this modern, western, feminist society bring to a marriage.

> Unless we can talk honestly about where half of the problems of marriage come from then we will only have half marriages.

The purpose of this work is not to denigrate your spouse but to inform you concerning the many sources of the problems effecting your marriage and God's solution for strengthening it.

Marriage is tough but always have been. The difference between marriage of old and now is that feminism and particularly modern feminism has rejected the role of the traditional wife and substituted in her place the feminist spouse. This change has led to the demise of marriage we experience today.

CHAPTER ONE

(The Current State of Affairs)

That your marriage is experiencing difficulties is not unusual. The U.S. marriage rate plummeted nearly 60% over the past 50 years. The marriage rate in 1970 was 76.5%, but today it stands at just over 31%. The average first marriage that ends in divorce lasts about 8 years the average second marriage that ends in divorce lasts a little less than 8 years.[1]

The seven top reasons for divorce are; Lack of commitment 73%, Argue too much 56%, Infidelity 55%, Married too young 46%, Unrealistic expectations 45%, Lack of equality in the relationship 44%, Lack of preparation for marriage 41%.[2]

I preside over a Saturday Morning Bible Study of men where the class suggests the biblical topic we discuss every month. Much interest was shown when the topic of 'difficulties in marriage life' was selected as the topic to be considered especially since 90% of the members have experienced divorce and approximately 75% of the men who were divorced have not remarried.

> The traditional role of the wife became unbalanced, and unattractive which resulted in her rejection of the traditional role.

In the western modern world the thought of marriage leaves a bad taste in the minds of the traditional man. It has become a Zero-Sum Gain[3] for us; our loss is her gain. Feminism has brought the modern woman to an inflection point[4] where she no longer relies on the woman's traditional role of marriage but now relies on feminism to define that role. Our female population has rejected the duties and values of the traditional female role of marriage while requiring that their mate retain the duties and values of the traditional male role of marriage. The modern western feminist spouse seeks fulfillment via employment rather than nest building. There was a time before the feminist movement that our women were trained to be wives from the time of their youth by their parents, church, and society. Young daughters set the table for the family dinner as her father set at the head of that table. Her older sister retrieved the plates of food from her mother in the kitchen and placed it before her father and brothers. Everybody remained silent as the father blessed the meal from the head of the table. Though as antiquated and repulsive this Norman Rockwell picture is today, it made sense back then because marriages were balanced. The father worked twelve hours days in a harsh and demanding workplace to provide a house for his family to live in and food for them to eat. His wife reciprocated by turning his house into a home, nurturing his children, and preparing their sustenance.

Now women are trained by their parents and society to be independent from men and financially self-sustaining by encouraging the acquisition of a college degree that affords them entry into middle management jobs, and egocentrism. For the modern woman marriage is all about their dreams and desires. When wives entered the workplace, the domain of what once was her husband's, became hers also, resulting in the transactional aspect of marriage becoming unbalanced. She began to bear too much of the load, caring for the nest and providing an income. The traditional role of the wife became unbalanced, and unattractive which resulted in her rejection of that traditional role. That dissatisfaction was Satan's path that feminism took to enter society and destroy God's model for marriage and hence the source of your displeasure.

The Root of Your Spouse's Masculinity

It is this shift in the psyche of women that is the foundation of this inflection point in modern, western, marriages we see today. This inflection in our modern society took root as far back as 1965 as an effort to spur the economic growth in the western world. Husbands and wives now have to maintain separate homes doubling the spending required to maintain just one home.

For example in the late 1960s, after more than a decade of success with positioning Marlboro as a masculine brand, Philip Morris decided to appeal to women through a new brand of cigarette; Virginia Slim, a 100-mm "slimmer than the usual" cigarette with the slogan "You've come a long way, baby". After a while they changed their slogan in the mid-1990s to "It's a woman thing" seeking to take advantage of and support for the evolution of the women's movement that promoted woman's self-sufficiency.

Consider Hearst's Publishers most valuable property and longest-running title 'Cosmopolitan'; it was first introduced in 1886 as a family magazine before transitioning in the 1970s under Helen Gurley Brown[5] to become the sexy women's "Cosmo" of today. It changed from a family magazine to an advertisement rich piece of fiction featuring short fiction pieces and advice-oriented articles on relationships, sex, fashion, entertainment, and careers. They promoted the modern feminist theme of "women should have the right to decide for themselves without society setting standards for them." And the removal of those standards gave birth to the Sexual Revolution in the 1960's and the promiscuity it promoted, this was right in line with the promiscuity of modern feminism today.

The culture was also influenced by the entertainment industry. T.V. shows transitioned from 'Father Knows Best' where Jim Anderson lead his family from an authoritative father figure to 'I Dream of Genie' where the woman is all powerful but still subject to her husband, to 'Mary Tyler Moore' show where the woman doesn't have a husband but fulfills her purpose in the work place, to 2 years later 'Maude' she represented the desire for women to be taken seriously, not only for their political views, but also to be taken seriously in the public sphere. Police Woman debuted in 1974, at last a woman with real power in the public sphere, then Charlie's Angels showed women working together to overcome evil men then 'la finale terminée' in 1998 'Sex and the City' where four single women live happy, promiscuous, sexual lives unencumbered by the social norms of matrimony.

You are experiencing problems with your marriage because God's design for it has been co-opted with feminist's redesign of marriage. The traditional wife has been replaced with the modern spouse and that by the promotion of media. When have you ever seen a commercial where the woman is portrayed as childish, weak, and inept? No, just the opposite, she is always portrayed at the sensible, wise, strong, and mature half of the marriage where she has to manipulate her husband from doing childish things. So successful was this programming of your spouse that she has devalued the worth of her husband.

> You are experiencing problems with your marriage because God's design for it has been co-opted with feminist's redesign of marriage.

The evidence of this truth is revealed when she doesn't value anything you have to say. Think that is not the case, how often does she interrupt you before you finish your thought? If you don't think your spouse has been affected by this phenomenon then you must reject the major premise of advertising: Ads work by using psychology to influence the way people think and feel about a product or service. Marketing seeks to develop a product people want, advertising seeks to develop a want people don't need. Feminism has masterfully worked both ends of this equation to the detriment of your marriage.

<u>Crooked Chair in a Crooked Room</u>

Studies on cognitive psychology research on field dependence show how individuals locate the upright in a space. In one study, subjects were placed on a crooked chair in a crooked room and then asked to align themselves vertically. Some perceived themselves as straight only in relation to their surroundings. To the researchers' surprise, some people could be tilted by as much as 35 degrees and report that they were perfectly straight, simply because they were aligned with images that were equally tilted. But not everyone did this: some managed to get themselves more or less upright regardless of how crooked the surrounding images were. Bombarded with warped images of their humanity... women tilt and bend themselves to fit the distortion.[6]

Culture is the crooked room your spouse was placed in and everything in that culture concerning her was off kilter, screwed, and, warped to the point that she can't perceive up from down or that she is out of alignment. In her mind the problem is not that she out of alignment but you are out of alignment with everything in her crooked world.

> Culture is the crooked room your spouse was placed in and everything in that culture concerning her was off kilter

Somehow or another feminism got your spouse to align herself with a crooked world and of course there is nothing straight about her. 1 Peter 3:7 speaks of your spouse as the 'weaker vessel' this is what that means; feminism has deceived your spouse into wanting to work a 40-60 hour week. Feminism tells her this is her 'best life' but what feminism doesn't tell her is that the natural desires God placed in her could not be replaced with a job. Though her boss has her working like a plantation slave still she wants to be married and have children. Feminism didn't tell her how to work on a job while being a wife and mother, it just redefined being a wife and mother as slavery, something the patriarchy pushes on them. Feminism tells them that their freedom from marriage and motherhood is where their best lives live. Now having bought into feminism's lie their lives are off kilter, they are confused and disillusioned and unhappy. Nothing is better for nor can remove God's plan for a woman from her nature. No job will ever remove her desire to be married and have children. Feminism just mounts the stress of a job on top of being married and having children. Just how stupid a lie Satan can get us to follow when God's marriage plan called for the wife/ mother to be taken care of by her husband. All her provisions came from his labor which set her free to do the things she was designed to do and loved to do; just be a wife and a mother. But having added a job on top of being a wife and mother has left everybody unhappy and unfulfilled. Both the husband and his children miss the benefits of having a wife and mother building a nest for them. But most of all she is unhappy, unfulfilled, exhausted, her nerves have been shattered and worst of all she can't seem to understand why her marriage is a mess and her life is a disaster; must be her husband's fault she surmises.

God speaks to spouses who have followed the lies of feminism with the same words He speaks to husbands who have followed the lies of feminism by requiring their spouses to work.

- Rom. 12:2 Do not conform to the pattern of this world, but be transformed by the renewing of your mind. Then you will be able to test and approve what God's will is—his good, pleasing and perfect will.

Because of the effects of modern, western, feminism men are calling marriage into question. The male experience of marriage in the western culture has been so unsatisfying to men that over the last 50 years there has been a 60% drop in marriages in the U.S.[7] God created women to be connected to men, this is why normally women express a passion to be married. Marriages have dropped 60% not because women all of a sudden stopped wanting to be married, marriages have dropped 60% and climbing because men don't want the product the modern woman is offering. Now I know as traditional husbands you feel you made a mistake in choosing your modern spouse and wish you could get away from her scot-free[8] well you can't because your bad choice for a mate has some ramifications you may not have thought about.

A Warning to Men Contemplating Divorce

Men take divorce much harder than women. For men facing a divorce or who have gone through the process, ending one's life might be seen as a way to remove one's self from the emotional and financial turmoil of divorce.[9] The Centers for Disease Control and Prevention reports that divorced men are eight time more likely to commit suicide than divorced women. Divorced men also often suffer from depression, anxiety and reduced self-esteem. The nature of men is not given to developing friendships and thus men have a smaller support network to help them combat depression, anxiety and reduced self-esteem – in fact, for many men their immediate family, meaning wife and children are the only emotional support they have.

If you or your spouse are dropping hints that a divorce is imminent then beware of the male warning signs of suicide. The CDC has a list of warning signs for men:

- Says he feels like a burden
- Becomes isolated
- Shows increased anxiety
- Says he feels trapped or in pain
- Shows increased substance abuse
- Shows increased anger and rage
- Has unusual mood swings
- Expresses hopelessness
- Sleeps too little or too much

- Talks about wanting to die, accesses information about death or makes plans for suicide

If you are going through a divorce, don't but still seek an honest divorce attorney, his revealing of just how one-sided marriage law favors the woman will do more for you to attempt to fix your marriage than most marriage counseling. And because of the trauma you are experiencing via your bad marriage professional Christian therapy may save your life.

The symptoms of an unhappy husband are:

- He starts excessive drinking
- Spends more hours at work, not wanting to go home
- Distant and more removed from his spouse
- Doesn't participate in family activities
- Depression

If you are experiencing these symptoms don't be so quick to blame yourself, the fault may lie on a disappointing marriage. Fixing your marriage may remove all the symptoms you are experiencing turning you into a better man.

<u>God's Design for Marriage</u>

In spite of all that Christian marriage is a beautiful thing. God created mankind in order that mankind might experience God's love for them, for God is Love and the prime directive or modus-operandi of His kingdom is that 'we love one another'. God created marriage so that both husband and wife might experience that love for one another in a relationship like none other.

The Greek language (the language of the New Testament) has four major words for love:

- Agape: Means actively doing what the Lord prefers, to wish well, to take pleasure in, long for; denotes the love of reason, esteem.

- Eros: physical or sexual love
- Philia: is the basis for a deep, lasting connection that we share with our closest friends.
- Storge: It's the result of living together day after day and settling into each other's rhythms.

These four aspects of love is only found in matrimony. This is the high estate, the unmeasurable worth, the total fulfillment of bliss a marriage that fulfills God's aspiration for it experiences.

The Experience of the Modern Marriage

I know bliss is not the word you would use to describe your marriage today, no, nothing close to it. But what happened to the bliss you experienced during your honeymoon. The same thing that happens to every man after their honeymoon. When I was young and unmarried Deacon Floyd explained it to me like this, he said, 'Son, every woman serves the boy she is interested in marrying from her shelves in front of the store but after she marries him she serves him from the wares in her store room. He then went on to explain to me that the things she will present to me at the beginning of the courtship she got from the items that had been cleaned and shined up, in other words 'made presentable' in the front part of the store where the potential buyers linger but after the marriage she will present to me things from her store room where the items are un-kept, not shiny, nor bright and new but dusty, old, and worn. Though I didn't listen I found this to be true, have you?

In car sales marketing this is called 'the old bait and switch trick' by now you know it well, where she advertised herself as a great catch but what you took home was not what she advertised. Bait and switch is illegal in all areas of commerce except one, matrimony.

Now speaking of your spouse, not to beat a dead horse but one more example, when a car-salesman has a car with a worn out engine that smokes he increases the weight of the oil and adds a stop smoke additive to the damaged engine. When you bought the car it didn't smoke but after a while of driving it does. The repair will be extensive but what are you to do, you're stuck with it. You can't sell it because no one will buy it and you can't junk it because you paid too much for it, you can't walk away from it because the bank still wants you to pay for it.

You got a lemon and in all your efforts to make lemonade you found that the juice was not worth the squeeze. You thought you married a good lemon but what happened to your lemon that turned it bad; into what most women of our culture are; feminists?

<u>Feminism: Lemonade without Sugar</u>

Feminism has encouraged women to seek equality at the workplace and modern feminism encourages women to view marriage as suppressive, while nowhere in feminism does it encourage women to experience God's intended love for marriage. This lack of feminism to recognize the longing for love God has placed in all of us is one of the many reasons for its decline.[10] This total rejection of God's aspiration for marriage has led to feminism's decline in the western culture. Though in western cultures feminism is on the decline its effect on your spouse is not.

> The Modern Feminist woman has removed the sweetness a wife brought to the marriage.

The Modern Feminist woman has removed the sweetness a wife brought to the marriage and replaced it with just the opposite of sweetness; selfishness, uncooperativeness, and non-commitment.

Though your spouse has made you feel that you are the reason your marriage failed or is failing[11] there is a very good chance that is not true. What causes marriages to fail is divorce and 70+% of divorces are filed by women that is unless your spouse has a college degree then that figure rises to 90+%.

Most likely you are not the blame for your marriage failing, let me say that again, most likely you are not the reason your marriage is failing because you didn't file for divorce. Just because you have the responsibility to manage your marriage because you are the leader you didn't have absolute control over your spouse, she has her own free-will that not even God will violate.

Back in Genesis God created the perfect environment for both Adam and Eve. God said of it:

- Gen.1:31 Then God looked over all he had made, and he saw that it was very good!

Even though God created the perfect environment for Eve it still wasn't good enough for her, she still thought the grass was greener on the other side. She still thought she had better options. If God couldn't make her happy with what He offered her then what makes you think you can?

> Even though God created the perfect environment for Eve it still wasn't good enough for her.

When your spouse filed for divorce it most likely was for 'irreconcilable differences' which is a legal way of her saying you didn't make her happy. It is not the leader's job to make his wife happy because that is an impossible task, only she can make herself happy. If she is not happy with the demands of marriage you can't make her happy with them. If she is unhappy with the sacrifices marriage calls on her to make you can't make her make those sacrifices. On all accounts Tom Brady was a good man, he supported his family from playing football, something he did all his life. He was married to Gisele for 13 years and they had two children.

He was playing football before they were married and no doubt his success at what he did was a significant part of what attracted her to him. He decided to play one last season of football before he retired and this made his spouse Gisele 'unhappy'. Because of her momentary unhappiness with his decision to extend his professional career one more season she dropped him in divorce and sought happiness elsewhere, it has been rumored she sought happiness from her ju-jitsu instructor. Imagine that, this woman traded in her husband of 13 years and the father of two of her children because he no longer made her happy. If Tom couldn't make her happy what makes her think her ju-jitsu instructor will? Your error in managing your marriage is you probably tried to make your spouse 'happy' instead of being the leader of your family. Though a woman may chaff under, she still respects and expects strong leadership from her husband but she will despise cowardice in him.

<u>Not Understanding a Woman's Physiology Leads to Disappointment</u>

Living with a woman and not recognizing the signs of her hormone swings is like living with a female Rottweiler and not recognizing what it means when her hair stands up on the back of her neck.

Women are moody and subject to the swings of their hormones. Women cry five times as much as men and who doesn't know to give them a wide berth when their menstrual cycle comes. From the start of their menstrual cycle until menopause their feelings are on a roller coaster. Unless she has commitment to marriage as part of her vocabulary her emotional swings will leave your marriage to her on the edge of divorce.

Millions of women experience symptoms of the menopause every day, but unfortunately we still don't fully understand all of the physical, emotional and mental effects it may have. There does however, seem to be a correlation between menopause and divorce rates. Before the recent changes to the law, divorce solicitors often found that women were citing symptoms of menopause as the reason for the breakdown of their marriage.

Additionally, the many symptoms of menopause have been known to have drastic impacts on the state of relationships. It causes an increase in disputes, a lack of understanding, reduced physical intimacy, poor communication and eventually the breakdown of a relationship.

Many women experience dryness in the vaginal area as well as an increase in infections that can make sexual activities more painful. Additionally, menopause causes a decreased libido which can make physical intimacy unappealing. When this occurs, it can be confusing for both men and women in a relationship and reduce the amount of intimacy shared between the two. This can be incredibly stressful and hard to understand.

As well as the physical effects of the menopause, it can have a big impact on mental health. Menopause has been known to cause anxiety, depression, trouble remembering things, and even a loss of concentration. These symptoms can be difficult to manage and accept, reducing the women's confidence in herself and her abilities, particularly if she is unaware that it is menopause that is causing these effects.

In the time leading up to menopause, there are many symptoms that women experience that may encourage the relationship to breakdown. Perimenopause can cause mood swings, depression, and trouble sleeping, to name just a few of the many symptoms that may be experienced. All of these things can lead to changes in the relationship dynamic. Reduced communication, confusion, and increased irritation can be the catalysis that causes a relationship to break down. The symptoms of menopause can make her more irritable, less likely to communicate, and confused. It may highlight current issues within the relationship and make them more challenging, or cause both individuals to feel isolated.

Many feel like they are quick to anger during the menopause and find there are more disputes within the relationship as both parties try to navigate through the new dynamic. This increase in conflict within the relationship can grind at the intimacy and emotional connections that have been built. Without effective communication and understanding, this can negatively impact the whole relationship.

A large percentage of women who initiate divorce are over 40 years old, the same age at which many start to experience perimenopause symptoms. This does not necessarily mean that menopause, perimenopause and divorce are connected, however they may contribute to each other.

In particular, perimenopause and menopause can lead to a loss of intimacy and sexual intercourse, which can make couples feel distant from each other. Additional strains due to changes in the relationship can lead to mistrust, a lack of understanding, and growing frustration.

Symptoms of menopause may not be the sole reason for divorce, but they are often a contributing factor. Open and honest communication is essential for a relationship to navigate through these difficult times.[12]

Aside from low energy levels, hormonal imbalances can also affect the way you feel. Emotions often encountered include irritability and sadness. Changes in oestrogen levels can adversely affect the release of chemicals such as dopamine and serotonin, which prevents you from feeling happy.[13]

In particular, perimenopause and menopause can lead to a loss of intimacy and sexual intercourse, which can make couples feel distant from each other.

The transition phase before menopause is often referred to as perimenopause. During this transition time before menopause, the supply of mature eggs in a woman's ovaries diminishes and ovulation becomes irregular. At the same time, the production of estrogen and progesterone decreases. It is the big drop in estrogen levels that causes most of the symptoms of menopause. Although the average age of menopause is 51, menopause can actually happen any time from the 30s to the mid-50s or later.[14]

Unhappiness in the modern woman is the harbinger of divorce. This is why God tells you to live with your wife in an understanding way because neither you or her know why she is acting so poorly, just understand that at times she will. And during those times spend time discussing your feelings with your spouse during therapy. And inquire concerning hormone replacement therapy or HRT and antidepressants. According to Centers for Disease Control and Prevention during 2015–2018, 13.2% of adults used antidepressants in the past 30 days. Use was higher among women (17.7%) than men (8.4%). The percentage of antidepressant use increased with age, from 7.9% among adults aged 18–39 to 14.4% for those aged 40–59 to 19.0% for those aged 60 and over.

Don't think that you can reason with her, she will run rings around you because women are verbal, they love to talk. Men love to contemplate. If you both are sitting together quietly she will interrupt your contemplation by asking you "what are you thinking." By the time you figure out just what you want to say she has already taken over the conversation. Her menopause never produce positive feeling only negative ones, the ones that make her blame you for all her displeasure.

Don't get mad, upset, or disappointed just be prepared to suffer through it, after all it's not her fault it is just biological.

<u>Why is it Important to Establish Paternity?</u>

Since one of the goals of modern feminism is the embrace of promiscuity: the modern feminist sensing weakness in you is the same as a shark sensing blood in the water. Especially for the feminist, perceived weakness is followed by disrespect and disrespect will be followed by promiscuity. Most paternity test labs report that about 1/3 of their paternity tests have a 'negative' result. Of all the possible fathers who take a paternity test, about 32% are not the biological father. But remember, this is 1/3 of men who have a reason to take a paternity test.

<u>Why Should You Establish Paternity?</u>

Establishing paternity is vital for all parties, especially your child. Once you have established paternity, several rights of the child are established. First, the child has more financial security because you are documented as the father. The child also can receive life, health, and Social Security benefits. Plus, your child can receive an inheritance from you.

The child will also understand what his or her parentage is. This might seem insignificant when the child is young. However, knowing the medical history of the father can help the child to take action to avoid problematic medical conditions that are inherited.

Of course, the child also should simply know who his or her father is. Even if the child is not interested in having a relationship with the father, knowing his name can be personally beneficial later in life.

Establishing who the father is, is essential for the parents. Legally recognizing how the father is connected to the child allows the two to build a father/child relationship. This can happen without establishing lawful paternity, but <u>you will no longer need the mother's permission to see the child</u>. Having the legal recognition establishes your rights and ensures the child will receive the necessary financial support...[15]

Paternity can be established without a D.N.A. test by signing a voluntary acknowledgment of paternity form, usually called VAP or VAoP. This form is for biological fathers to establish their parentage by signing this form or affidavit. Though a man may choose to seek genetic testing prior to signing the VAP form, no state requires you to do so.

<u>Women Are Predisposed Towards Marriage</u>

God created the man to care for Earth, He created the woman to be with the man. Women are predisposed to want marriage because marriage or attachment to a man is their God given purpose. Men desire to be married because it is not good that a man be without a wife.

- Gen. 2:15&18 15 The Lord God took the man and put him in the Garden of Eden to work it and take care of it... 18The Lord God said, "It is not good for the man to be alone. I will make a helper suitable for him."

The end result of the wedding bouquet and the garter toss are revealing today. The tradition is that whatever woman caught the wedding bouquet was next to be married, the same as with the men, whoever caught the garter belt was next to be married. Women still jockey for position to catch the wedding bouquet but the men do just the opposite, they seek to avoid even being touched by the dreaded garter belt. Ask an unmarried woman if she wants to be married and the preponderance of times she will answer 'yes'. Ask an unmarried man if he wants to be married and the preponderance of times he will respond to the question with a 'pause'. He is not sure of the answer because today's modern woman bring so little to the table while at the same time expects the man to bring a traditional husband.

Women are not only biologically programmed to desire marriage but marriage is also their greatest benefit as a woman, especially in these times where the divorce laws favor them with a life-long income via alimony and child-support. They also get to satisfy that hunger an empty womb craves in them. Feminism allows your spouse to crave marriage but not commitment to marriage. In her mind she has the children she craved and the financial support from alimony and child-support so what does she really need you for if you are not making her 'happy'? You are dispensable and replaceable so when she divorces you doesn't mean she stopped wanting to be married. Even before she divorced you she is assuming she can do better than you.

Your spouse's rejection of God's aspirations for your marriage is the inspiration for this work. God clearly instituted a model for marriage and modern feminists has totally rejected it. The bad news is most men of our time and culture struggle to adapt God's model of being a traditional husband in our marriages while the modern feminist seek to at all cost to destroy God's model.

Stop being pissed off, you dealt those cards you have to play them

You wanted a wife but because she had no idea that by definition a wife is selfless all she really wanted was a wedding, wedding ring, honeymoon, fabulous pictures to post on social media, you to impregnate her, and you fulfilling your role as the one to make her 'happy'. You gave her all these things and so she was happy and her happiness lasted until she had your children, then her unhappiness settled in along with your belligerence. Because you wanted the marriage to survive you held in there even though she was unhappy and you were belligerent. You both put a good face on it for a while but after a while the wounds you both were inflicting on each other were becoming too deep to bear. Because you didn't make her 'happy' she felt she dealt herself a bad hand while at the same time you threw in the cards of ever being happy with your marriage. Stop being pissed off, you dealt those cards you have to play them. But the good news is God has spoken to our plight. We married out of ignorance, God's first instruction to us is to stop being 'ignorant'.

<u>God Doesn't Address Fault He Addresses Solution</u>

- 1 Peter 3:7 You husbands in the same way, live with your wives in an understanding way, as with someone weaker, since she is a woman; and show her honor as a fellow heir of the grace of life, so that your prayers will not be hindered. (NASB)

In God's instruction He doesn't ascribe fault but ascribes solution. In 1 Peter 3:7 He addresses what the husband is to do to repair his marriage, not what he has not done to damage it and in this work we will do the same. In this work we will discuss what God wants you to do to repair your marriage not what you have done to damage it. I'm sure you have already heard enough of that. In all societies women are given a pass but men are told to man-up and carry the load. The faults of men are screamed to the highest decibels in professional media, social media, all forms of entertainment, and standard cultural discourse. But an analysis of the woman's faults are kept as hidden as the Secret Service keeps hidden our national secrets.

Contrary to the screaming's of your spouse, you did not marry the perfect woman who because of your bad behavior changed into a lousy wife. She was lousy to begin with and so were you. That is a given so no need in either calling the kettle black.[16]

So God commands husbands to 'live with your wives in an understanding way'. That statement assumes that you have not been living with your wife in an understanding way. What does to 'live with your wife' mean? And what is an understanding way? To 'live with your wife' includes among other things that you address the problems of your marriage. That you have a problem with your marriage is evident, also evident is that you do not have an understanding of the problem because you still have the problem. How can you 'live with your wife in an understanding way' if you don't address the problem and how can you address the problem if you don't understand the problem? If you have not understood the problem what then have you been addressing? Have all your efforts been for naught? Has the juice not been worth the squeeze? If so then there is much God has commanded husbands to do but here is a novel idea; let us first do what God recommended that we as husbands do first, UNDERSTAND!

<u>Understand What?</u>

Understand the root and exasperation of the problem with your modern, western marriage. No two marriages are identical but to a greater or lesser degree they are alike; they all suffer from the effects of sin and reap the influences of what the culture has sown.

The problem is two-fold, the curse of Gen. 3:16 which is the root of the problem:

- Gen 3:16 (NLT) Then he said to the woman, "I will sharpen the pain of your pregnancy, and in pain you will give birth. And you will desire to control your husband, but he will rule over you."

Much will be said of this problem later, <u>wives seeking to rule their husbands.</u> This problem is exasperated by the mindset towards marriage the modern/western/feminist women promote.

Feminism took women out of the home and placed them in the workplace. This changed the family dynamic. Women took unto themselves the masculine role of provider along with it a desire to rule over the husband. This social reconstruction of marriage in the western world erased the traditional marriage. Your spouse is one who rejected traditional marriage and desired to reconstruct marriage to please the modern feminist woman as stated below.

'Without socially constructed expectations, marriages could be happier and more successful. We'll never know unless we start working to make it less of a phenomenon when couples go against the grain. It would be cool to throw out some outdated traditions, start our own new ones and see the effects that could have on marriage success.'[17],[18]

Later in this work we will show the disastrous effects of feminist's socially reconstructed marriages. Now since today there is no lack of expression in society of the women's viewpoint of the problem with marriage this book is written from the husband's vantage point as to the problem (supported with statistics) and from God's point of view as to its solution (supported with scripture) for marriages gone astray.

Though there are nuggets sprinkled throughout scripture and this work will consider many of them, God's answer to the deflated and defeated husband today is primarily found in two areas of scripture though God has so much more to say in other passages.

First Peter 3:7 "Husbands, live with your wives in an understanding way, showing honor to the woman as the weaker vessel, since they are heirs with you of the grace of life, so that your prayers may not be hindered".

And

Ephesians 5:25-28 Husbands, love your wives, just as Christ loved the church and gave himself up for her 26to make her holy, cleansing her by the washing with water through the word, 27and to present her to himself as a radiant church, without stain or wrinkle or any other blemish, but holy and blameless. 28In this same way, husbands ought to love their wives as their own bodies. He who loves his wife loves himself.

CHAPTER TWO

(The Curse)

<u>The Root of the Problem</u>

The Book of Genesis is the book of beginnings. In the beginning God who is already existing because He has no beginning created everything that begins. And everything that He created was 'good', including not only all things material but also His rules of conduct the citizens of His creation were to obey. This would lead to a peaceful, prosperous, and joyful existence where mankind could live in the experience of God's love for them. But mankind having been created in the image of God were given the right to decide for themselves rather to obey God or not, they decided to not obey God's 'good' rules which resulted in 'bad'.

But you ask 'since God knew that man would choose to disobey God rather than obey Him, why did He give man a choice? Good question, God is love and He desires the man He created to experience that Love. Love, loves to be requited if not then love becomes defiled. Love can't be coerced it must be given freely. Man must decide to love God out of his own free-will therefore he must be afforded the choice to obey God or not. Now you ask 'what does obedience have to do with love:'

- John 14:15 "If you love Me, keep My commandments."

If you love God then you will trust Him enough to do what He says.

If you love God then you will trust Him enough to do what He says. One's love of God is based on one's trust of God. I do what He says because I know that He loves me and only asks me to do what is best for myself because He loves me. In the same way a wife should obey her husband because she trusts him and he has validated her trust by requiring of her only those things that benefit her first spiritually and then physically. Love is based on trust.

Peter had boasted that he would never forsake Jesus but he did so Jesus asked Peter three times if he truly loved Him.

- John 21:15 When they had finished eating, Jesus said to Simon Peter, "Simon son of John, do you love me more than these?" "Yes, Lord," he said, "you know that I love you." Jesus said, "Feed my lambs." 16Again Jesus said, "Simon son of John, do you love me?" He answered, "Yes, Lord, you know that I love you." Jesus said, "Take care of my sheep." 17The third time he said to him, "Simon son of John, do you love me?" Peter was hurt because Jesus asked him the third time, "Do you love me?" He said, "Lord, you know all things; you know that I love you." Jesus said, "Feed my sheep.

Jesus was giving us an example of fulfilling John 14:15 'If you love Me, keep my commandments'.

Okay back to the issue at hand, man decided not to obey God and like a weed that grows man's disobedience immediately sprouted forward and began to choke the life out of all the 'good' God had created. First Eve then Adam rebelled against God's lordship over His kingdom and the bad seed of that weed bore fruit which resulted in both the man and his wife seeking to rule over each other.

Now man was not created to rule over the woman neither the woman over the man but they both were created to rule over Earth in a harmonious union. Gen. 1:26-28:

- Then God said, "Let Us make mankind in Our image, according to Our likeness; and let them rule over the fish of the sea and over the birds of the sky and over the livestock and over all the Earth, and over every crawling thing that crawls on the Earth." 27So God created man in His own image, in the image of God He created him; male and female He created them. 28God blessed them; and God said to them, "Be fruitful and multiply, and fill the Earth, and subdue it; and rule over the fish of the sea and over the birds of the sky and over every living thing that moves on the Earth."

The verb 'rule' in this passage does a lot of work, it doesn't mean to 'lead' but 'to have dominion'.

- Rule: מָשַׁל
- Transliteration: mashal, phonetic spelling: (maw-shal')
- Definition: to rule, have dominion, reign

They both were created to have dominion but not over each other. But when the man sinned by disobeying God when he ate of the forbidden fruit he gave sin a foothold to enter the world God created for them. This was an 'inflection point' that led to all the world's problems. In like manner feminism was the foothold that Satan used to enter matrimony and create the many problems you are experiencing.

Disobeying God never leads to a good end and that is evidenced by God's plan for a harmonious marriage going askew. Instead of both the man and the woman exercising dominion over God's Earth <u>they both would have to live not in harmony with the Earth but in conflict with it and each other</u>. Isn't that what you are experiencing in your messed-up marriage, a lack of harmony leading to an abundance of conflict as you both seek to rule over each other?

Since the woman plays the long-game of nagging have given up on exercising leadership, the very thing you should not have done? Giving up your leadership to your spouse is the very door to all the problems your marriage is experiencing. Disobeying God always leads to a world of unanticipated problems. God never intended for you two to dominate each other but since the fall of Adam and Eve where domination was brought into marriage when Eve sought to dominate Adam God reversed that sin so that Adam should now dominate Eve. Eve, like your spouse, wasn't taking this laying down but resisted Adam's leadership by seeking to usurp his authority, in the same manner as your spouse.

- Gen. 3:16b ... And you will desire to control your husband, but he will rule over you. (NLT)

<u>This is not a One-sided Problem</u>

Both men and women suffer from being under the curse of Gen. 3:16-19 therefore there is enough blame to apply to both husband and spouse.

- Then he said to the woman, "I will sharpen the pain of your pregnancy, and in pain you will give birth. And you will desire to control your husband, but he will rule over you." 17To Adam he said, "Because you listened to your wife and ate fruit from the tree about which I commanded you, 'You must not eat from it,' "Cursed is the ground because of you; through painful toil you will eat food from it all the days of your life. 18It will produce thorns and thistles for you, and you will eat the plants of the field. 19By the sweat of your brow you will eat your food until you return to the ground, since from it you were taken; for dust you are and to dust you will return."

Since the woman exercised dominance over the man when she lead him into disobeying God's command not to eat of the tree of the knowledge of good and evil, God now will curse the man to exercise dominance over his wife and curse the woman to desire to dominate her husband.

The mutually interdependent relationship the Lord had created was replaced with a desire for one spouse to rule the other.

The mutually interdependent relationship the Lord had created was replaced with a desire for one spouse to rule the other. Sin had wrought discord, the battle of the sexes had begun. Both man and woman would now seek the upper hand in marriage. The man who was to lovingly care for and nurture his wife would now seek to dominate her, and the wife would no longer desire to be a support to her husband but desire to wrest control from him.

<u>The Challenges of Your Marriage are not Your Fault Alone</u>

Neither condition existed before sin. Adam was given the mission to care for the Earth and Eve was to assist him. But just as sin ruined everything on Earth God's desire for there to be harmony in the marriage was also ruined.

God created the man first then created the woman to be an assistant to the man. God placed man at the head or leader of his family under the same understanding that He placed man over the Earth; so that he would be responsible for caring for his family like he was responsible for caring for the Earth.

God operates with order not disorder and establishes a hierarchy not for the leader to 'dominate' all those beneath the leader but for the leader to 'care for' those who fall under his umbrella of care, provision, and protection.

Christian husbandry equals caring for, providing for and protecting all the members of his family. But the curse instituted oppression and self-centeredness:

- The Hebrew word for rule is מָשַׁל (dominance) = oppression and self-centeredness

God established Christ like leadership because when the leader imitates Christ the leader will edify all those under his care. But because of the curse leadership became domination whose attributes are demonic because domination will destroy all persons who dominate and are dominated over. This is why God speaks of the relationship between the man and his wife now being cursed.

The struggle to master over each other was not a command from the Lord but a statement of fact, both shall attempt to rule (מָשַׁל-dominate) over each other.

This curse represents a retaliatory justice. Eve manipulated her husband; she would now be manipulated by her husband. Adam chose to be ruled by his wife now he will desire to rule/dominate her.

<u>The Response to the Challenges of Your Marriage is Your Responsibility Alone</u>

Much light emanates from the words 'desire' and 'rule' when compared to their use in Gen. 4:6-7:

- 6Then the Lord said to Cain, "Why are you angry? Why is your face downcast? 7If you do what is right, will you not be accepted? But if you do not do what is right, sin is crouching at your door; it <u>desires</u> to have you, but you must <u>rule</u> over it."

The word 'desire' / תְּשׁוּקָתוֹ / phonetic spelling: tesh-oo-kaw' / definition: a longing is the same word used of Eve in Gen. 3:16b ... And you will desire to control your husband, but he will rule over you."

In the same manner as Eve desired to rule over Adam by encouraging him to disobey God and obey her by eating the fruit of the tree of the knowledge of good and evil, sin laid in wait to sneak up on Cain with the desire to rule over him BUT God's warning to Adam,

Cain, and you as a husband (must) rule over both the woman's and sin's desire to control you.

This task to not let sin rule over you is an impossible task outside of the help of the Holy Spirit. He leads, guides, encourages, and empowers you to have victory over sin. To get the Holy Spirit's help you first must get Jesus Christ by placing your trust in His payment for your sin. When you rely on Jesus Christ to cleanse you from your sin and not on your own efforts to cleanse your sins then Jesus Christ not only removes the punishment of your sins but places you under the umbrella of His own righteousness which establishes a new relationship with God. You are no longer considered an enemy of God but His child. Your sins are removed as an impediment to God's presence and His Holy Spirit begins the work of sanctification in your life. This work of sanctification is a work that transforms you into something that resembles Jesus Christ in all His perfections. That transformation will be hindered or assisted as you decide how much you will or will not obey His prodding's. This is why the scriptures encourages us to stop grieving, quenching, and resisting the Holy Spirit.

<u>Your Spouse Will Be Your Greatest Challenge</u>

Now Satan will use every tool at his disposal to get you to grieve, quench, and resist the encouragement of the Holy Spirit and often times your spouse will be used as one of those tools. Job's wife gives us an example of how Satan will use your spouse. After Job was greatly used by God to put Satan to shame by proving that Job didn't serve God because of the enormous blessings God had given to Job. Not only after God allowed Satan to remove those blessings He also allowed Satan to inflict devastating illness on Job's body and when even then Job didn't turn against God, Satan played his hold-card: Job's Wife

- Job 2:7-10 So Satan went out from the presence of the Lord and afflicted Job with painful sores from the soles of his feet to the crown of his head. 8 Then Job took a piece of broken pottery and scraped himself with it as he sat among the ashes. 9 His wife said to him, "Are you still maintaining your integrity? Curse God and die!" 10But he said to her, "You are speaking as one of the foolish women speaks. Shall we actually accept good from God but not accept adversity?" Despite all this, Job did not sin with his lips.

The biggest impediment you will have to establishing a godly marriage will often be your spouse. Just as Satan used Job's wife at his most vulnerable condition Satan will use your spouse when God calls on you to take a stand for Him. In the same manner as Satan used Job's wife to hinder Job as he stood firm in honoring God your spouse will hinder your attempt to stand firm in the godly leadership of your home. When this happens don't give up heart but pray and continue to be God's man in your home.

> The biggest impediment you will have to establishing a godly marriage will often be your spouse.

Now what are the tools a woman uses to resist the rule of her husband and to rule over her husband; sex, shame, guilt, insult, whining, and shear disobedience. The <u>withholding of sex</u> in a marriage is a go-to for women even though the bible clearly warns against it.

- 1 Cor. 7:3-5 The husband should fulfill his marital duty to his wife, and likewise the wife to her husband. 4The wife does not have authority over her own body but yields it to her husband. In the same way, the husband does not have authority over his own body but yields it to his wife. 5Do not deprive each other except perhaps by mutual consent and for a time, so that you may devote yourselves to prayer. Then come together again so that Satan will not tempt you because of your lack of self-control.

The spouse who closes the door to sex opens the door to Satan.

She successfully uses shame because a man's ego is directly related to how he is perceived by others. His standing in the eyes of his family, friends, co-workers, society in general, and especially his wife speaks to his own self-worth. Nothing takes the life out of a man more than the disrespect of his spouse.

When she <u>insults</u> him she will tell him things like how happy 'Tom, Dick, or Harry wives are because they remodeled their kitchens'.

She uses <u>shame</u> when she tells him that she expected more out of him and she should have listened to her mother who told her you would never be able to meet her needs. That she had better get use to doing without because if she married you she could not depend on her parents to give her the things she wants.

She will use <u>guilt</u> when she reminds him that they would have had enough money to remodel the kitchen if he hadn't supported the Church with a special offering for some evangelists whose ministry fell on hard times. In other words 'it his fault because of the bad decision he has made'.

Her <u>need</u> to be right will not allow her to listen to reason, she can't hear you say 'let's save up the money first so we don't have to add to the bills we're already having difficulty paying". She believes she will cook more home meals because of the new kitchen but you know after a week she will return to her not cooking.

<u>Whining</u> needs no explanation for after a while of 'I want a new kitchen, I can't cook in this old kitchen, you don't love me if you don't give me a new kitchen'. Soon the nagging will drive you crazy and you will do anything just to shut her up. So let's take a look at one classic example scriptures uses to warn us against giving into the demands of a nagging wife; Sampson and Delilah:

- 15Then she said to him, "How can you say, 'I love you,' when you won't confide in me? This is the third time you have made a fool of me and haven't told me the secret of your great strength." 16With such nagging she prodded him day after day until he was sick to death of it. 17So he told her everything. "No razor has ever been used on my head," he said, "because I have been a Nazirite dedicated to God from my mother's womb. If my head were shaved, my strength would leave me, and I would become as weak as any other man." 18When Delilah saw that he had told her everything, she sent word to the rulers of the Philistines, "Come back once more; he has told me everything." So the rulers of the Philistines returned with the silver in their hands. 19After putting him to sleep on her lap, she called for someone to shave off the seven braids of his hair, and so began to subdue him. And his strength left him.

When she can't get from you what she wants she takes matters into her own hands and places a down payment with a kitchen contractor in direct disobedience to your decision. You come home from work one evening and you find two men tearing out your old kitchen. You look at your wife and she tells you she got tired of waiting for you and took matters into her own hands.

<u>What Type of Man Are You Too Your Spouse?</u>

> You determine how she responds to you. She will go as far as you let her because you are the leader.

It is important that you know what type of man your spouse sees you as and as important you must know what type of man you are. Because women by nature are responsive, your spouse takes her que's from you, you determine how she responds to you. She will go as far as you let her because you are the leader. If you allow her to 'sissify' you then you will be unsatisfied with and embarrassed by your marriage.

During the Viet-Nam War I volunteered for the Illinois National Guard to escape the draft. I did my basic training in Fort Polk, Louisiana. The drill sergeants were brutal, they demanded respect because if they didn't the recruits would get out of hand and the lack of training to survive in a war situation could jeopardize the whole war effort. But when I finished my training in Fort Polk they shipped me back to my home base which was in Chicago. There things were different. One day the whole battalion was called to assembly and when the First Sergeant addressed the troops of his company they responded by telling him to shut-up. The disrespect they showed him instantly revealed to me that this was just a mickey-mouse operation and I responded accordingly. A first-sergeant has infinitely more authority than a drill-sergeant but if he doesn't exercise it then he by default leads his company of men to disrespect him. In the same sense you are the leader of your family but if you don't exercise your authority your spouse will disrespect you and your children will laugh at you. Everyone aware of your dysfunctional marriage will accuse you of being pussified and rightly so.

An Alpha Male:

Alpha males are the clear leaders in their marriages. They have a direction they want their families to be headed and a path for their marriages to take. They are confident husbands, reassured, and realistic. They are committed to the wellness of their family and will rise up to challenge any perceived threat to it. Though they will seek and listen to their wives opinions by taking her desires and concerns into his calculation he will never allow her to boss him. Because of the Genesis curse his wife will attempt to rule over him but his steadfastness in his leadership role, accompanied with his wise-godly decisions, will keep his wife submissive to him. This is the type of husband all women desire and respond too as wives, they will not respond to such a husband like a spouse.

Sigma Male:

Sigma males are best characterized as 'lone-wolfs'. They can turn a deaf ear to distractions, including their spouses. They don't have a deep level of commitment because they just don't care enough to deal with problems. They are more introverted and not amp to tell their spouses what they actually think. Come what may they go on about their business and will welcome their spouses if they want to come along with them. They are viewed by their spouses as unemotional and uncaring. Their spouses were attracted to them because they came across as 'distant and mysterious' but the frustration and demise of their spouses self-worth soon causes her to regret her marriage to him.

Beta Male:

A Beta male is passive, subservient, weak, and effeminate. They go along to get along with their spouses because they are intimidated and afraid of losing them. They are the good guys that finished last. You often find them in a woman's friend-zone. Women marry them after they have tired of the abuse received from the bad-boys and Chads they subjugated themselves too. Beta males generally end up with the women who have been emotionally damaged, and impregnated by the Chads and Pokies of the world. These women readily become bored and dismissive of their beta-husbands. Because of the Genesis curse they walk all over them, belittling them at every turn. Their children don't respect them because their mothers don't. Their spouses will cut them down like the winter wheat and all they love will go to the wind like its chaff.

As you can see the only type of husband a woman wants is the Alpha Male and the type of man God wants you to be is an Alpha-Husband. The further away you are from displaying the attributes of an Alpha-Husband the greater will be your marriage troubles. Take an honest account of what type of husband you have been so you can know what changes you need to make to become the Alpha-Husband your spouse wants and needs. As you change into an Alpha-Husband your 'spouse' will reciprocate by changing into a 'wife'.

> Your spouse will tell you which type of husband you are by how she treats you.

So which type of husband are you? Your spouse will tell you which type of husband you are by how she treats you. Is she idolizes and respects you, then you are an Alpha-Husband but if she is broken, distant, and unaffectionate, then you are a Sigma-Husband but if she is disrespectful and dismissive, then you are a Beta-Husband. This old-saying is true 'you can tell the type of man a husband is by looking at his wife'.

<u>Satan's Bag of Tricks to Destroy Your Marriage</u>

What are the tools Satan uses to rule over both husband and wife; lust of the flesh, lust of the eyes and the pride of life.

- 1 John 2:15-17 For all that is in the world—the lust of the flesh, the lust of the eyes, and the pride of life—is not of the Father but is of the world.

Now let us consider how Eve fell prey to Satan:

- 1Now the serpent was more crafty than any of the wild animals the Lord God had made. He said to the woman, "Did God really say, 'You must not eat from any tree in the garden'?" 2The woman said to the serpent, "We may eat fruit from the trees in the garden, 3but God did say, 'You must not eat fruit from the tree that is in the middle of the garden, and you must not touch it, or you will die.' " 4"You will not certainly die," the serpent said to the woman. 5"For God

knows that when you eat from it your eyes will be opened,
and you will be like God, knowing good and evil."

Eve's mistake was that she listened to Satan as he highlighted what God had restricted (the fruit from the tree of the knowledge of good and evil) and not on what God had permitted (every fruit from the trees of the garden but the fruit of the tree of the knowledge of good and evil). But why didn't she listen to her husband who was standing right there as Satan was leading her astray? Because he said nothing, when your spouse is complaining about something she doesn't have, remind her of all the things you have provided for her. Adam made many mistakes; first, he stood by and said nothing, second, he allowed his wife to be influenced by Satan, third, he allowed his wife to misquote scripture (God did not say "and you must not touch it, or you will die." Fourth, he allowed Satan to lie to his wife by contradicting God (You will not certainly die). The scriptures say 'A little leaven leaveneth the whole lump' so it is with your spouse, a little displeasure will lead to displeasure in the whole marriage. Don't let any statement of displeasure go unanswered.

Adam was created first and in God's order that made him the leader of his wife Eve. You as the husband is the leader of your wife. In the same way that Satan sought to influence Eve this modern, western, feminist culture has influenced your wife. Don't be like Adam and do nothing, your marriage, family and self are at stake. God advises you to live with your wife in an understanding way and as with the weaker vessel (1 Peter 3:7).

She like you is prone to succumb to the socialization of this godless society but you are the leader and therefore responsible to intervene in the socialization of your family by leading them in a godly direction. This work was produced for those who have not.

- Gen. 3:6 When the woman saw that the fruit of the tree was good for food *(lust of the flesh)* and pleasing to the eye *(lust of the eyes)*, and also desirable for gaining wisdom *(pride of life)* that is to be like God knowing good and evil, she took some and ate it. She also gave some to her husband, who was with her, and he ate it.

And so what was the effect of Adam's failure to intervene? Sin entered the world and the full effect of sin broke loose on him. Sin is not going away, like God told Cain, "you must rule over it".

Our marriages are a mess because we don't live with our wives in an understanding way knowing that they are the weaker vessel subject to succumb to the socialization of this modern feminist culture. We not only must know her but we are also to love her (Eph. 5:21-25) with a love that places her edification above our own.

> All wives innately want their husbands to be the leader of their family but their pride will offer up resistance.

This is much easier to say than to do and because we don't stand our ground when they push-back on our leadership, we instead tend to blame our spouses for taking the lead not remembering that God has told us to rule over them as they seek to rule over us.

As a side note: all wives innately want their husbands to be the leader of their family but their pride will offer up resistance. Breaking a woman's pride is almost as difficult as breaking your own but with a righteous lifestyle coupled with prayer 'all things are possible with God.'

<u>Jesus' Example of Defeating Satan</u>

Satan tempted Jesus in the same way that he tempted Eve in 1 John 2:15-17, the lust of the flesh, the lust of the eyes, and the pride of life.

In the Gospel of Luke 4:1-13 we see Satan tempting Jesus;

- The devil said to him, "If you are the Son of God, tell this stone to become bread." 4Jesus answered, "It is written: 'Man shall not live on bread alone.'
  - This temptation aimed itself at 'the lust of the flesh' but unlike Eve who saw that the fruit was one good to the taste Jesus instead responded to Satan's temptation with the Word of God, He said "it is written, man shall not live by bread alone".
- Then again we see Satan tempting Jesus; 5The devil led him up to a high place and showed him in an instant all the kingdoms of the world. 6And he said to him, "I will give you all their authority and splendor; it has been given to me, and I can give it to anyone I want to. 7If you worship me, it will all be yours." 8Jesus answered,
  - This temptation was aimed at 'the lust of the eyes'. Jesus again didn't respond like Eve did and say 'it is pleasing to the eye' but responded using the Word of God. He said "It is written: 'Worship the Lord your God and serve him only.'
- And again we see Satan tempting Jesus 9The devil led him to Jerusalem and had him stand on the highest point of the temple. "If you are the Son of God," he said, "throw yourself down from here. 10For it is written: " 'He will command his angels concerning you to guard you carefully; 11they will lift you up in their hands, so that you will not strike your foot against a stone.'
  - This temptation was aimed at 'the pride of life' because if Jesus threw Himself off the temple heights He would be saying that no matter what He did, God would protect Him.
  - Now the pride of life is Satan's go to when all else fails. It is his most powerful tool to trick you into

not following God's advice because Satan failed to conquer his own pride to his demise;

- Isaiah 14: 12-15 How you have fallen from heaven, morning star, son of the dawn! You have been cast down to the Earth, you who once laid low the nations! 13You said in your heart, "I will ascend to the heavens; I will raise my throne above the stars of God; I will sit enthroned on the mount of assembly, on the utmost heights of Mount Zaphon. 14I will ascend above the tops of the clouds; I will make myself like the Most High." 15But you are brought down to the realm of the dead, to the depths of the pit.

- But Jesus answered "It is said: 'Do not put the Lord your God to the test.'"

<u>The Takeaway of Jesus' Example</u>

Satan surmised that Jesus would be weak because He had not eaten for 40 days and 40 nights. What Satan did not consider was that during those 40 days and 40 nights Jesus was praying and fasting which resulted not in weakness but in strength.

This is an important lesson for you to lay hold of because for you to correct the wayward direction of your marriage you will have to 1. Depend on the Word of God, 2. Pray and fast, 3. Set aside your pride. Setting aside your pride is the most difficult obstacle to a godly marriage you will encounter because to love your spouse in the midst of her betrayal will require you set your pride aside. But if you do these three things like Jesus did then Satan also will leave you alone until he finds a more opportune time. What is the more opportune time for you to fall prey to Satan?; when you stop depending on the Word of

God, stop praying and stop fasting, then it will be impossible for you to restrain your pride?

- 13When the devil had finished all this tempting, he left him until an opportune time.

> The more a husband and his wife set their pride aside the better and more loving their marriage will be.

I contend this that the more a husband and his wife set their pride aside the better and more loving their marriage will be. What brings despair to Satan's eyes is when he sees husbands and wives setting aside their pride. And what puts the glint of glee in Satan's eye is when he hears either the spouse or the husband say '"I'm not happy". Now my greatest failure in my marriage was when I said to myself "I deserve better than what my spouse was giving to our marriage". I was not 'happy' and I'm sure it showed but nowhere in Genesis do you ever find God saying He created man and woman to be 'happy', no, He created them to work together, have children, care for each other, and be committed to each other. When either you or your spouse makes 'happiness' a goal of your marriage be assured you are headed for divorce.

<u>Why Don't God Just Give Me Peace in the Midst of My Miserable Marriage?</u>

Genesis 3 gives us the proper view of God. When Adam and Eve sinned, God did not strike them dead on the spot, as His holiness and justness alone did require. Nor did He say, "That's okay, don't worry about it," as His love alone may have desired. Rather, God dealt with their sin as a serious matter. He imposed the penalty their sin required but He interposed His grace, so that the fallen couple could be restored to fellowship with Him. In Genesis there is both the curse and the covering for their sin. These verses teach us that God allows us to suffer consequences of our sin but also He provides salvation from sin's final judgment; total and eternal separation from God. The beginning of this separation is seen in what Adam and Eve were found doing right after they sinned.

- Gen. 3:6 When the woman saw that the fruit of the tree was good for food and pleasing to the eye, and also desirable for gaining wisdom, she took some and ate it. She also gave some to her husband, who was with her, and he ate it. 7Then the eyes of both of them were opened, and they realized they were naked; so they sewed fig leaves together and made coverings for themselves. 8Then the man and his wife heard the sound of the Lord God as he was walking in the garden in the cool of the day, and <u>they hid from the Lord God</u> among the trees of the garden. 9But the Lord God called to the man, "Where are you?" 10He answered, "I heard you in the garden, and I was afraid because I was naked; so I hid."

They were afraid because Adam had been warned:

- Gen. 2:16 And the Lord God commanded the man, "You are free to eat from any tree in the garden; 17but you must not eat from the tree of the knowledge of good and evil, for when you eat from it you will certainly die."

They hid from God because they feared death, nothing has changed in all these years, those who don't have Christ fear God because He has the power of death in His hands. But Adam and Eve didn't physically die that very day. But yes they did die because the death spoken of here is not defined as physical death but spiritual death that is a separation from God which is seen in their hiding from God. But God comes looking for them, not to punish them but to save them from punishment. It is on this side of the grave that God comes looking for you to save you, it is on the other side of the grave that God comes looking for you to punish you.

<u>Cloth your Marriage in God's Grace</u>

Your marriage is spiritually dead and as long as your marriage is separated from God you will never experience the joy a godly marriage brings. I know that you have been doing your best but your best has not nor ever will be enough.

> Your marriage is spiritually dead and as long as your marriage is separated from God you will never experience the joy a godly marriage brings.

Now follow the picture here, when Adam and Eve disobeyed God they realized that they were naked. Well weren't they naked all the while? Yes and No. They didn't have on any cloths but in their sinless state they were clothed with God's glory. What do you mean by that? In Psalms 8 the Psalm that praises God for His majesty in verses 4 and 5 we get to eavesdrop on a couple of angels as they wonder about man at the time God created them. Listen to what they ask each other as they are bewildered.

- What is mankind that you are mindful of them, human beings that you care for them? 5You have made them a little lower than the angels and crowned them with glory and honor.

Now the word 'crowned' is עֲטַר, transliteration: atar, phonetic spelling: aw-tar', definition: to surround. They are not crowned with God's glory in the sense that they own it but they are surrounded by it. They were in essence clothed with God's glory so they were not naked. But after they sinned God's glory would no longer surround or cloth them because they were no longer fit to wear it. Sin had removed God's glory in the same way as sin in your martial relationship has removed God's glory from your marriage.

No method that you devise will restore God's glory to your marriage only the removal of sin. How do I know this? Continue to observe the picture in Genesis.

- Gen. 3:7 Then the eyes of both of them were opened, and they realized they were naked; so they sewed fig leaves together and made coverings for themselves.

Why did they sew fig leaves to cover themselves, because God's glory no longer 'surrounded' them. They wanted to cover up their nakedness because it revealed the absence of God's glory. Their attempt to cover their sin with fig leaves is the same attempt you make to cover up your marital discord. It will never do, only by bringing Jesus into your marriage will it ever be clothed with God's glory. How do I know this? Observe how God dwelt with the problem of being naked before Him.

- Gen. 3:21 The Lord God made garments of skin for Adam and his wife and clothed them.

An animal was sacrificed to provide garments of skin, I believe it was a lamb because of what John the Baptist proclaimed when he saw Jesus approaching;

- 29The next day John saw Jesus coming toward him and said, "Look, the Lamb of God, who takes away the sin of the world! (NIV)

God's provision to cover the nakedness of our sin is the sacrifice of the One who is sinless and who stands before God's judgment in our stead. Jesus Christ the Righteous. Jesus shed His blood to cover our sins and if we are to be saved then all we have to do is trust in God's provision, Jesus the Christ. In like manner if you want your marriage to stop suffering the effects of sin then clothe it with the blood of Christ. What do I mean by that? Bath you marriage in all that Jesus, the Word of God has to say. In this work much more concerning what Jesus has said will follow.

Your marriage is messed up because like Adam and Eve and every culture after them including this one we are living in is hiding from God, afraid of Him naked and ashamed.

This work is not for those of you with godly marriages but for those of us who have acted shamefully and ruined our marriages, both male and female. Your marriage is experiencing difficulty because sin is not just an act but it originates from a condition and like DNA that condition passed on to every generation after it because sin was found to abide in its original host Adam.

> We experience the toil and pain of unsuccessful marriages because we didn't cover our marriages in God's wisdom,

We experience the toil and pain of unsuccessful marriages because we didn't cover our marriages in God's wisdom, Jesus Christ is God's Word and His Wisdom. The good news is that it is never too late to make a change in how you manage your marriage. If you would have it to become successful then successfully follow Christ. This will not be easy.

In Genesis 1:28, the couple was commanded to be fruitful and multiply, and to subdue the Earth. That command involved work, but not toil and pain. But now God introduces toil and pain as the necessary price to fulfill these primary roles.[19]

But you may ask 'why does God require toil and pain?' Toil and pain is the necessary consequence of disobeying God. Everything God made was good, including the structure and order of the family. Any deviation from that 'good' can't lead to 'better' but only toil and pain. God as Creator of the Universe and King over His Earthly Kingdom has the responsibility to insure that they; all of His creation operate according to His dictates. A kingdom where sin is left unpunished devolves. God in His mercy doesn't intervene into the natural effects of sin, this so that His children will experience those negative effects and thereby be detoured from committing acts of disobedience. When God's children are obedient to God's dictates then His Kingdom prospers and His children experience the joy of existing in fellowship with Him. When you stop taking the advice of the ungodly, and the dictates of your spouse but in faith start trusting in God's marital directions for you as His leader of your family then you will start to see a change in your marriage and the joy you were entitled to experience will begin to take hold. The juice will become worth the squeeze.

CHAPTER THREE

(The Exasperation: Modern Feminism)

If the curse found in Genesis 3 where husband and wives both seek to dominate each other were not bad enough the problem you are experiencing in your marriage is being exasperated by Modern Feminism.

When God created man and woman He in all His wisdom assigned to them certain roles to function by. Today we call these roles 'traditional'. The feminists in our modern culture vehemently reject this role and define it by such terms as 'suppressive' and 'slavery' and 'regressive'. But as we have said before any deviation from God's design doesn't lead to 'better' but to 'bad'.

If your wife is less than seventy-five years old she to a greater or lesser degree has been infected with feminism. And the struggle you had or are having with her in your marriage to a large degree finds its foundation in the Genesis curse but lately is being exasperated by the feminist mindset. The effects of the curse has been in effect since Genesis chapter three but the role of women in marriage has only be under attack since the advent of feminism. So just what is feminism?

<u>The Buzzword for Feminism is Equality</u>

<u>Traditional/Actual feminism</u>: is vastly different from Modern Feminism. The former developed in the late 1800's through the early 1900's. It was a movement that sought for women to be treated as equal to men. Such political issues included women's suffrage, equal pay, equal employment opportunities, etc. This quest for equality of social rights led to the homogenization of husband and wife's roles in marriage we began to see take effect around the year 1965.

Feminism is basically bipolar because although women were created to desire the leadership of a husband, feminism all the while teaches them to resist that leadership because they feel male leadership is patriarchy.[20] This bypolarism in her thinking has caused confusion in yours and lead to dysfunctional marriages. Men desire traditional wives because they desire to be traditional husbands.

The error of feminism is the lie that women becoming masculine will better fulfill their purpose. Women were never created to be masculine but to be their husband's helpers, this basic flaw leads to abuse of husbands and the discord you are experiencing in your marriage.

In Democracy in America (1835), Alexis de Tocqueville observed that the Americans had "carefully separated the functions of man and of woman so that the great work of society may be better performed." He concluded that "if anyone asks me what I think the chief cause of the extraordinary prosperity and growing power of this nation, I should answer that it is due to the superiority of their women." He saw that the family "was presided over by the American woman, the model of Christian principles of sacrifice, duty, and compassion."

Feminism began the work of destroying that 'great work of society' and <u>modern</u> feminism has advanced that work of destruction by creating an environment that is the worst place in the world and all of history to choose a wife from. No other culture of men on planet Earth wants our women, feminism has turned them into men and we like Adam when Satan deceived his wife stood by and did nothing as she headed off to corporate America and gave her best not to your family but to her boss.

Now Satan is the shrewdest creature God ever made (Gen. 3:1) and his appetite for destroying anything God has sanctioned is unbounded. Satan focused his deadly aim at the first family by attacking the woman and he has not deviated from his method. His not being satisfied with the level of destruction feminism wroth he upped the ante with modern feminism.

<u>Modern Feminism</u>: Its development was during the 1960's. The core philosophy was anti-God, anti-authority, anti- just about

everything! ... modern feminism also claims the existence of a patriarchy even with the US society. This means they claim all women are victim to a systematic form of oppression.[21]

> Your spouse considers you her oppressor, no wonder she resists your leadership.

How about that, your spouse considers you her oppressor, no wonder she resists your leadership. You were thinking she was just bull-headed, full of her own ideas but all the while lying just beneath the facade of conversation her feminism harbored resentment. Your leadership in her mind hinted of oppression or as feminists term it 'patriarchy' which to them is anathema and every restriction on a woman's desire is oppression. While the traditional definition of feminism speaks on gender equality it has always been from the female perspective. Traditional Feminism has morphed into Modern Feminism which is a guise for entitlement. It encourages women to do what they want, when they want and how they want, without any restrictions placed on them by the patriarchy. As such we see the devolution of the female, her family and her marriage. You thought you were getting a partner, someone you could work with towards the common goal of a future not knowing that in the feminists mind 'the future is female'. You didn't marry a partner you married an adversary, something that became evident not long after you said 'I do'.

Marriage and family if not anything else is defined as Alexis de Tocqueville observed sacrifice, duty, and compassion not entitlement. Modern Feminists promote 'toxic masculinity'. This trait establishes a type of bypolarism in women because women were designed to love and cooperate with their husbands but modern feminism has encouraged women to place their economic goals above their sacrifice for family. Instead of remaining in their femininity (a softness and cooperation with men) men became the 'enemy' and his desires for a traditional wife became evil.

A man's greatest desire is cooperation from his wife but the modern feminist describe a husband's desire for cooperation as toxic masculinity. As such marriages are broken and strife in marriages is abundant. How often have you in your marriages resisted entering into a conversation with your spouse about an idea or direction you want to take the family in because you know her push-back will be emasculating. This is why God said in Gen. 3:16 you must rule over your wife or she will rule over you. We as men have been too weak in our fortitude to grasp hold of and retain the leader's role in our families. Women respect and expect their husbands to be strong all the while the truth of Gen. 3:16 plays out in her desires. This truth is revealed in social media today where women praise themselves for being strong and independent but express the desire for a strong man who can ride roughshod over their pig-headedness and settle them down.

In the old west some cowboys were bronco-busters, their job was to mount onto a wild horse and ride it until the horse gave out. The Bronco-buster portrays a rugged cowboy character fighting to stay aboard a rearing, plunging bronco, with a stirrup swinging free, a quirt in one hand and a fistful of mane and reins in the other. Unless he stayed on top of that bucking bronco it would never be of any use to the man. When feminism tells your spouse she is strong, independent, and don't need no man, when she buys into the delusion she secretly wants a strong husband to take control of her and the family. She will reject and replace a soft man whom she has 'sissified'.

When it comes to being the man of your house God calls on you to be a bronco-buster; one who has not been sissified[22] by his spouse but at last we turned out to be nothing but a tenderfoot, a greenhorn, unaccustomed to the rough ride of marriage. In the beginning marriage was not intended to be a rough-ride but since the curse and the advent of modern feminism marriage has proved to be quite the ball-buster.

In the Observer it is stated that women made a well-intended, fairly simple but admittedly consequential swap when we were fighting for equality. We gave up our feminine side so we could attain what we saw as masculine goals: the corner office, the big promotion, freedom. And we started acting less like ladies and more like lady bros. Don't get me wrong, these are fantastic objectives, but we didn't have to 'man up' to get them. Feminists started using the word 'girly' as if it were a bad thing. In a more humanized era, men loved girly—and so did women. Now, it's a full blown insult. Women mistakenly coveted what men had, rather than holding onto the uniquely feminine power we had. We abandoned it and did it their way. Not exactly empowering. Femininity (not feminism) has always been a huge source of female power, so why were we discouraged from embracing it?[23]

A Later Effect of Modern Feminism

> The husband has become as replaceable to his modern spouse as her many former lovers were.

Modern Feminism promotes promiscuity; women seeking to live their 'best lives'[24] by having a high body-count results in tremendous psychological damage.[25] The husband has become as replaceable to his modern spouse as her many former lovers were. The higher a woman's body-count the higher her divorce rate.

- Women with 10 or more partners were the most likely to divorce.
- Women with 0-1 partners were the least likely to divorce.

Of the rare times a man files for divorce the two main reasons are: infidelity and lack of appreciation. The IFS shares that approximately

13% of married women report cheating on their spouses. <u>Women ages 18-29 appear slightly more likely than men of the same age to be guilty of infidelity in a marriage.</u> Married women report their highest rate of infidelity in their 60s. Married women are about 15% more likely to report having emotional affairs than men.[26]

Modern Feminism spawned the hook-up culture[27] and since the raise of modern feminism around the time of the Baby Boomer Generation that generation did not follow the Greatest Generation: Born 1901-1924 and the Silent Generation: Born 1925-1945, whose mandate for its females was to at all costs keep family together. That emphasis changed for the feminists of the Baby Boomer Generation's to 'keep making me happy or I will divorce you!' This degradation increased in every generation since the Baby Boomers also seen in the Generation X: Born 1965-1980, Millennials: Born 1981-1996, and Generation Z: Born 1997-2012. This change of emphasis for the modern feminist 'keep making me happy' has morphed into 'accept and do everything I want' or I will feel oppressed by your masculinity. This attitude has led for the most part to promiscuity, masculine demeanor, self-centeredness, and the lack of appreciation for the husband's contribution to the family and society.

Modern Feminism spawned a new slang word 'ratchet'.[28] Modern Feminists are like free-range horses, they are wild and uncontrollable whereas a man requires peace, structure, and discipline in his home these women roam unstructured and undisciplined. These wild horses require a stern hand because the more a husband simps for them the more ratchet she becomes because her ability to control him is the attribute she disrespects the most in him. The more she controls you the more she will disrespect you!

This assessment does not apply to every individual female in all the different generations but speak to the vast majority in each generation. And not every woman will be affected to the same extent by this poison but all women will be affected to a certain degree; some greater some lesser. You must ascertain just how much your spouse is infected and adjust your response accordingly.

Some wild horses require a bronco-buster to tame them and some require a horse-whisperer[29] it just depends on how much your spouse has been affected by modern feminism. The husband whose wife will receive a soft word will always make for a more peaceful marriage than the husband whose spouse bucks him at every turn.

> Some wild horses require a bronco-buster to tame them and some require a horse-whisperer it just depends on how much your spouse has been affected by modern feminism.

Even in the midst of our modern feminist culture there are still a few women who have the stuff of wives who understand their role as keeping the family together and assisting her husband as he guides the family towards spiritual maturity. But they are a rare and precious jewel about as rare as a godly husband who puts the care, provision and protection of his family above his own care, provision and protection.

<u>The Failure of Older Women to Teach the Younger Women</u>

In my Tuesday Morning Bible Class I teach a class primarily, though not exclusively made up of older women. When it comes to the injunction of Titus 2:5 two things often come to my mind; 1. Would the younger women listen to the older women and 2. What would these older women teach them? In this western culture of ours age is not given deference and maybe that is a good thing because I'm not sure Titus 2:3-5 would come to the minds of the older women. After all when I consider what the older women taught their children, your spouses, it was that men should be feared and girls should get an education so that they can survive financially after their husbands abandon them.

Your spouse should have been taught by her mother and the older women of the church. In answer to my first question above the younger women will listen to the older women if the older women lived revenant lives or lives that emanated what is sacred to God and if they were sober minded women and stopped being malicious. Specifically, the older women should teach and encourage the younger women in the church by word and by example. And in answer to my second question above, that when they teach they teach what was 'good'. And the good that they were to teach is found in the seven injunctions of Titus.

- Titus 2:3-5 (NASB) Older women likewise are to be reverent in their behavior, not malicious gossips nor enslaved to much wine, teaching what is good, 4 so that they may encourage the young women to love their husbands, to love their children, 5 to be sensible, pure, workers at home, kind, being subject to their own husbands, so that the word of God will not be dishonored.

They were to teach the young women to be (1) lovers of their husbands; (2) lovers of their children; (3) self-controlled; (4) pure; (5) work from home (building their nests); (6) kind; and (7) subject to their husbands.

There was a time when the things above we commonly taught to women so that you would not have to be a bronco-buster but could enjoy the peace that a horse-whisperer enjoys, but not so much now.

In Major League Baseball in the last inning when the game is on the line and a slow runner is on first base the club manager will substitute a pitch-runner to take the place of the slow runner. Today in our modern culture women have deemed the men to be slow-runners and have taken their place in the family. They have removed the husband off first base and taken his place. Now having taken his place and not knowing how the game is played they don't run straight to second base, then third, then home, no they run to the outfield then to the pitcher's mound then take a break in the dug-out then back to first base. As a man have you ever just watched your spouse complicate a simple thing and wonder just how her mind works? It doesn't work like yours. As you deal with her, the weaker vessel, picture a single train track proceeding straight and uninterrupted continuing straight unto its destination that is your brain. It understands a problem and devises a straight path to the solution. Now picture a railway junction with a multitude of tracks all crisscrossing heading to destinations unknown that is your spouse's brain. It wants to run to the outfield and the dug-out at the same time. It wants to obtain a Ph.D. during her most fertile and attractive years after which she wants to climb the corporate ladder during the last years of her fertility and beauty then after her beauty and fertility have faded she wants to obtain a husband paying no concern to the fact that while she was her most attractive and useful to a man she gave herself to feminist lies. And because of hypergamy she wonders why no man of her stature will marry her but complains how there are no good men left or that all the men want younger women. God understood that we are both easy to get things wrong and so made both our roles simple. Her role is uncomplicated, it is spelled out in Titus 2:3-5 above. But feminism has convoluted everything pertaining to women. Nowhere in Titus 2:3-5 does it speak about getting an education in case your husband leaves you with the kids, nowhere does it speak about being afraid of your husband, or living your best life. It is simple; love your husband, love your children, be under self-control, keep yourself unpolluted from the world, let your husband build you a house but you turn it into a home for him and your children, be a kind person, and let your husband lead the family. The husband's role is even simpler; provide, protect, and be his family's pastor. In Life Application Bible Commentary 1 & 2 Timothy and Titus they describe it as follows:

WHO'S ON FIRST?

Why did Paul stress that young Christian women should love their husbands and families? While such teaching may appear too obvious for mention, there are forces at work in today's world that undermine even that very basic part of family life. Today women are being told that their interests or desires come first, that they must seek what makes them happy before they can be good wives and mothers. While women should be encouraged to use their gifts and abilities, each Christian woman must align her priorities with God's wisdom, not the world's values. She must love her husband and her children, accepting the sacrifices that love brings. God will honor those who value what he values.

<u>Sacrifice the Fifth and the Other Six Will Follow</u>

> Have you become less of a man in her eyes because she depends less on you?

Do you desire the creature comforts of this generation more than you desire your wife to remain at home? Did you chose a woman that is comfortable with the level of provision you are able to provide or does both she and you crave the creature comforts that demand a second income? Is your spouse now suffering from struggling to divide her allegiance between her employer and her husband? Are you upset because she no longer appreciates you? Have you become less of a man in her eyes because she depends less on you? Your role as husband sits atop a three legged stool, Provider, Protector, and Leader, don't remove the leg of provider from that three legged stool for the sake of creature comforts. With the loss of your provider role you will soon discover that the loss of your role as leader will follow. The bible says it this way:

- Matthew 6:24-26 "No one can serve two masters. Either you will hate the one and love the other, or you will be devoted to the one and despise the other. You cannot serve both God and money. (NIV)

Love and hate in the above verse speaks of having to make a choice between the two. If she works she will chose her employer over her husband. If your spouse is more concerned about what her employer demands of her than what you desire of her then scripture is right and you should not expect of her to put your desires first in any aspect of your marriage.

Remove the wife from the home and the marriage will suffer. Women who work both in the home and on a job will experience the stress of a 96 hour workweek, not be attentive to their children nor their husband. Feminism cried for equality in the workplace at the same time they made no provision for the deleterious effects of removing the role of the stay at home mother. Compared to children who were cared for at home by their mother the children in the daycare were 63% more likely to experience stress. Out of those who did experience stress when being cared for outside of the home 40% had level of cortisol[30] high enough to indicate a stress response. These were very young children between the ages of 3-4.5 who were daily exhibiting a stress response. According to the American Psychological Association a long term stress response will affects all systems of the body including the musculoskeletal, respiratory, cardiovascular, endocrine, gastrointestinal, nervous, and reproductive systems. This is in no way ideal for a child's physical or emotional development, especially during such crucial and formative years.

<u>A Two Headed Anything is a Monster</u>

All people should have the same rights as others but the problem arises when equality is defined making no distinction between the separate roles of husbands and wives. <u>Husbands and wives are equal but their roles are different</u>, in the same way a pharmacist is equal to a doctor but their roles are different. A doctor can prescribe a medication that the pharmacist may deem problematic to the recovery of the patient. His concern will lead to a consultation between the pharmacist and the doctor who then may change the path to health the doctor was leading his patient. The pharmacist is not greater than the doctor, one is not greater than the other but each are needed for each has their own area of expertise and by working together their cooperation leads to the ultimate goal of the health of the patient. The husband's area is leadership, protection and provision the wife's is nest building, child rearing and family cohesiveness. As both husband and wife cooperate in their respective roles the family grows up healthy.

Since Modern Feminism is anti-God by which I mean it is arrayed against God's model of marriage that being; the husband is the leader of the family, not a dictator but one who also has a leader he is subject to; Jesus Christ. The wife nurtures the children and establishes the nest for the family (Psalm 31:10-31) all this done under her husband's leadership; the husband leads his wife as he is led by Christ's command to love his wife.

This concept is foreign to the modern woman of the western culture. Even though no organization of Earth functions without a leader. In every government, business, philanthropic society, animal kingdom, educational organization, etc. etc. etc. there is a leader. Your home is dysfunctional because your spouse is not equipped to lead your family all the while she refuses to follow your leadership.

It doesn't look good for your sons and daughters either. Not understanding the role of a wife in a Christian marriage the modern feminist will train their children to follow their model of feminism[31] which will lead their children's marriages to also end in divorce. Having divorced you now single modern feminist mothers will cling to their unmarried and divorced children instead of the husbands they divorced. Their children will become their life-long partners. This concept is called 'Husband-Son Hybrid'.[32] Feminism's path of destruction has endured these last 58 years with no end in sight.

More than half (51.2%) of all Black children lived with one parent in 2022, compared with about one in five (21.3%) of white children.

Academically speaking, children in single parent families are more likely to drop out of high school when compared to peers with married parents.

Experts are increasingly viewing child development disruptions through the lens of adverse childhood experiences (ACEs). These potentially traumatic events can take many forms, such as divorce or parental separation, poverty, mental health challenges, substance abuse at home, exposure to violence, and so forth. ACEs can cause "toxic stress," which can lead to lasting, deleterious disruptions in a child's physical and mental health, education and other life outcomes.

For the sake of our society your spouse needs Christian counseling.

<u>The Cry of the Modern Feminist</u>

The battle cry of the modern feminist is 'I don't need no man!' This attitude has led to the exit of men from the marriage pool. All across America, marriage, sexuality and relationships are on the steady decline among young people. According to a new Pew Research study, 63% percent of men aged 18 to 29 report being single. That means the number of single young men is nearly twice that of single young women, indicating a large breakdown in the social, romantic and sexual lives of American men.[33]

"The Marriage Crunch" a study by Harvard and Yale researchers that projected college-educated women had a 20 percent chance of getting married if they were still single at 30, a 5 percent chance at age 35, and just a 2.6 percent chance at age 40.

Aging feminists may have felt that they didn't need a man but the hunger of an empty womb and lack of prospect of finding a mate (hitting the wall) soon find them in line to have their eggs frozen. It is ironic that feminists who saw no value in men seek the sperm of destitute men who for $10.00 dollars will donate their sperm to sperm cryobanks. Aging feminists are now purchasing the right to reserve sperm at cryobanks because the supply of sperm is diminishing.[34]

The above is not a put-down of all women but is an observation of the general affects feminism has had on the women of our modern western culture. These observations are illuminated with the hope that you as a husband will better understand the motivations that, to lesser or greater degree, energize your spouse.

> He has provided a hope and a solution if you are husband enough to implement it.

What a dismal end the goals of modern feminism has achieved for western woman. And how tainted is the pool of women western men have to choose from. God is aware of the demise of the culture feminism has effected and His ears are not closed to the cries of godly men who want to be godly husbands. He has provided a hope and a solution if you are husband enough to implement it.

CHAPTER FOUR

(The Solution)

<u>First Understand Your Woman</u>

Genesis 3 tells us about how sin entered the world. It also shows you how sin enters your marriage. Adam and Eve chose to do what they knew was wrong. They chose themselves over God, and by doing that, they damaged themselves. And from that time onwards each and every marriage suffers from that curse. But God has given us the following revelation and by it we can be aware of the curse's destructiveness and with this knowledge we can cleanse each other of its defilement.

THE SOLUTION: Understand her and then Cleanse her with the Word

It is significantly more difficult to deal with a problem when you don't know its existence and origin. This is why in the first chapter we discussed the 'curse' and in the second chapter we discussed the 'exasperation' of the problem.

Now as to God's solution to the problem, the Bible instructs husbands to live with their wives according to 'knowledge'. Let's just be honest about it as husbands we did not live with our wives according to 'knowledge'. For most of us chapters one and two of this work were absent from our understanding. We 'lived' with our wives according to the individual expectations of both hers and ourselves. The foundation of those expectation were rooted in Disney Fairy Tales where you are the knight in shining armor and she is the damsel in destress. You make your entry into her life slaying her dragons and you both ride off to the castle 'living happily ever after'. It doesn't take long for either of you two to notice that marriage is less like a Disney Fairy Tale but more like a Greek Tragedy. Not understanding the problems illuminated in chapters one and two has lead the both of you towards frustration, anger, dissatisfaction and resentment. This resentment will lead to divorce and will destroy the family unit God is depending on to spread the knowledge of His Kingdom.

<u>God Says Husbands 'Understand' Your Spouse</u>[35]:

- First Peter 3:7 says, "Husbands, live with your wives in an understanding way, showing honor to the woman as the weaker vessel, since they are heirs with you of the grace of life, so that your prayers may not be hindered"

<u>Understand</u>: Gnósis "experientially know") – functional ("working") knowledge gleaned from first-hand (personal) experience, connecting theory to application; "application-knowledge," gained in (by) a direct relationship.

You can't understand your spouse by reading any book, let alone this one. Even the bible states in Jeremiah 17:9 "The heart[36] is more deceitful than all else And is desperately sick; Who can understand it? (NASB). 1 Peter is not telling you to understand your spouse, it is telling you to live with her 'according to knowledge' and this 'knowledge' is gleaned through firsthand experience of her. You can't see the wind you can only see the effects of the wind blowing things around or feeling its pressure on your body parts, in like manner you can't see your spouse's heart, her inner being but only it's effect on the things it comes into contact with. As you live with her you can see where her heart is and if it is not on you then you will not only see that but you will also feel it. The bible also says in Matt. 6:21 For where your treasure is, there your heart will be also. This application of understanding comes from a nuanced inspection of what she treasures.

> The difficulty you feel in showing love for your spouse is because as a feminist she does not treasure you in her 'heart'.

The difficulty you feel in showing love for your spouse is because as a feminist she does not treasure you in her 'heart'. She puts everything else before you; her job, her education, her friends, her children, her parents, her appearance, her me time, her acquisition of material things, etc. etc. etc. This is not an excuse it is just an explanation as to why you find it difficult to embrace the snake feminism has turned your spouse into. Even still God calls on you to treat her with 'honor', confusing I know but hang in there we will explain this command later on in this work.

<u>We Live in an Evil World</u>

Understand her so you don't expect more out of her than what is there. Your spouse suffers from an identity crisis, she thinks she is the leader in your marriage. Because she acquired this problem honestly, it wasn't her fault but our society that trained her to be this way, your responsibility is to recognize that she has a problem because you didn't marry a wife. When you signed your marriage contract the single woman you married changed her classification from single to spouse, not wife, that's what you got, a woman you are legally attached too. Therefore act accordingly out of love for her as she is. The bible doesn't say this will be easy but it is doable. First pray to God that He endow you with the strength of a husband. Then set aside your pride, we know you deserved better but you made her your choice so it's not a matter of what you deserve it is a matter of what you choose.

And so men therein lies the problem, we didn't know the field in which we had to choose a wife from had been seeded with feminist weeds. These women we have to choose from have been told that they are Independent Divas, Bosses and Queens (none of these things make for good wives).

Our mistake was that we paid no attention to God's first command in 1 Peter 3:7 to 'know our wives'. Had we actually believed God and followed His instruction we never would have married our spouses. We followed Satan's instruction for choosing a wife, we followed after the 'lust of our flesh and the lust of our eye'. And as is true to form Satan deceived us to our own destruction.

The things that men come to know they want most out of their wives are cooperation, a peaceful nest, as much physical beauty as possible, and a feminine demeanor. But what modern feminist offer is independent, contentious, overweight women, 30.4% of American women are obese, over 73% of U.S. adults overweight, the percentage of women who have severe obesity is 11.5%. These women come with fake body parts and a contentiousness that fights you at every turn. They offer you these things because they feel they don't have to consider what you want. They don't have to consider what you want because you approach them is such a thirsty manner you convey to them that you will accept them under any circumstances.

If you ask a modern woman what she expects out of her husband she will be able to write you a dissertation on the question but if you ask the modern woman what a husband expects out of her, she will draw a blank.

It doesn't take long for the physical beauty you were infatuated with morph into a middle aged woman that has worn you down and turned you into something even she despises; a 'weak man' who is not strong enough to tame her. Many of you have already experienced her next move; to divorce you and look for a 'strong man' that can tame her, but not necessarily in that order.

Around half (51.4%) of single mothers under 18 have never married, almost a third (29.3%) are divorced. About two thirds are

White, one third Black. Only one out of four African American women will ever experience matrimony.

If your spouse is of the Baby Boomer generation or later your spouse statically was not raised to be a wife because she came from a broken home where husband/wife dynamics were never modeled.

- Among adults with low incomes, just 26% are married.
- Irreconcilable differences is a buzz-word for "I'm no longer happy"
- People with low incomes are the least likely to marry, but they're also much more apt to substitute cohabitation for marriage (13%) than any other income group. They're also at greater risk for divorce (46%).
- Among working-class adults, 39% are married and 41% have been divorced.
- 56% of people with mid-and upper-class incomes are married and 30% have been divorced.
- The vast majority of divorces are initiated by the woman mainly because for the modern woman marriage is transactional, because she is materialistic she wants the highest earning man not the man who portrays the highest Christian character. Materialistic desires have never been a static component but one that soon outgrows your economic ability to satisfy.
- 70 to 90% of marriages are filed by the woman, this advantages them because as the first to file:
  - You get to say what the issues for the divorce are
  - The court reads your document first
  - Your lawyer speaks first
  - You get to tell your side of the of the story first
  - You set the time table for the hearing
- Since 1965 no-fault divorces, welfare (aid to dependent

children) alimony and child support has become prevalent.

- These statistics are bound to get worse as Generations X, Z, and Generation Alpha[37], replace Generation 'Baby Boomers'.

- Our culture has taught woman that the man is to be feared or used as a utility and when he no longer makes you happy he is replaceable or disposable.

  - The modern woman has never been taught that the object of being married is not to be happy but to raise and sustain a Christian family for the furtherance of God's Kingdom to His glory. In this pursuit a husband and his wife will obtain their greatest level of joy.

- Absent in the mind of the modern woman is that happiness dwells on materialistic, worldly pleasure while joy is derived from soul satisfying, emotional wellbeing. Happiness is considered an emotion, while joy is a state of mind. Happiness is merely external, and fleeting whereas joy is internal, selfless, sacrificial, and is derived from a spiritual connection with God.

- The modern woman believes marriage was instituted to foster happy lives, but God created the institution of the family to pass faith to the next generation so that the Gospel would spread to every corner of the Earth.

- The goal of modern feminism is for the woman to obtain 'happiness' but in her feminist method the woman will never obtain 'joy' and therefore never obtain what she truly needs; contentment, peace, satisfaction, and godly purpose.

Men like Johnny Depp, Tom Brady, Steve Harvey, Kevin Costner and, many more with all the material wealth they commanded could not make their spouses happy, so what chance do you have?

> Men are like dogs and women are like cats; a dog is made happy by a pat on the head and something to eat. No one knows what makes a cat happy!

Men are like dogs and women are like cats; a dog is made happy by a pat on the head and something to eat. What makes a cat happy? Take a moment and ponder the question. Can't come up with an answer, of course not because no one knows what makes a cat happy!

Even women married to women don't know what a woman wants, a truth established by the fact that lesbian divorce rate 73% is twice as high as it is for gay guys?

These are the issues you are dealing with in your marriage to a spouse who is not a wife. Let's just face it if we would have known about this modern, western, feminist woman we would not have gotten married to her in the first place but it's too late now so continue studying to see what God has to say;

- 1 Peter 3:7 "Husbands, live with your wives in an understanding way, showing honor to the woman as the weaker vessel, since they are heirs with you of the grace of life, so that your prayers may not be hindered"

<u>Live With Her in an Understanding Way</u>

To live with your wife in an understanding way is to gain knowledge of her through first-hand (personal) experience. Then connect the theory of God's words (knowledge) and its application to her (wisdom) via your direct relationship with her.

God has a path for each of us to follow and He has fenced in that path all along the way. That fence is His Word and as long as we don't jump over that fence and start walking along another path then we will be just fine but when we chose our spouse we jumped over God's fence and we followed another path that lead to the destruction we are experiencing in our marriages now.

You see there were a lot of things we didn't understand about her when we married her. This work is not designed to put her down but designed to give you understanding so you can 'live with her'. A problem is magnified 10 fold when you don't understand it but when you do you are better able to see it coming and avoid it altogether. God warned you from the beginning in Matt. 15:14 that 'If the blind lead the blind, both will fall into a pit.' Stop being blind then you will be better able to avoid the marital pitfalls and your marriage will become less burdensome because you have taken the time to better understand her.

> If you understood her you would stop expecting so much from her.

Also if you understood her you would stop expecting so much from her. You were expecting that she act like a traditional wife does, not understanding that she is not. When you understand that she has been influenced by our modern feminist culture you will be better able to see what motivates her. You will better understand what the bible means when it says 'for where (her) treasure is there (her) heart will be also'.

Live with your wife in an understanding way because she is the weaker of you two. Understand that she has been influenced by this modern, feminist, western culture. And as such you have your work cut out for you. Don't cut and run because she has devalued herself but because of God's command continue to treat her as something of value.

<u>Showing Honor to the Woman</u>

<u>Honor</u>: properly, perceived value; worth (literally, "price") especially as perceived honor – i.e. what has value in the eyes of the

beholder; (figuratively) the value (weight, honor) willingly assigned to something.

The husband should ascribes value to his spouse because she is God's daughter and He has shed His blood for her that she may have eternal life. Consider her someone worth cleansing so that she may fulfill the role of wife God has designed for you both to enjoy.

Also God did not choose her for you, you chose her for you and because you did you must value her. Though hidden and unrecognizable she has intrinsic value and it is up to you through prayer and implementing God's word cleanse her up so that you may realize her true worth.

In the same way as Adam and Eve chose to disobey God you chose a spouse not according to God's instruction and like Adam you have been cursed to work your field (your spouse) with 'toil' and 'pain'. The enemy (feminism) has snuck into your field and planted thorns and thistles, you must de-weed your field so that you may reap the blessing of her harvest.

In the same way a field overgrown with weeds doesn't devalue the field not as long as the farmer is not lazy but puts in the work of clearing his field of the weeds. You in the same way must also cleanse your spouse.

A godly husband will ascribes value to his spouse even in her weakened state. And because he has knowledge of her weakened state he will respond to her imperfections with consideration of her needs, desires, gifts, frailties, abilities and inabilities. A husband who acts on this knowledge of his wife will greatly enrich her life, as well as his own.

This husband understands the affect that this modern, western, feminist culture has on his spouse and reduces his expectation of her until he does the work on her God advises in Ephesians 5:25-27

- 25Husbands, love your wives, just as Christ loved the church and gave himself up for her 26to make her holy, cleansing her by the washing with water through the word, 27and to present her to himself as a radiant church, without stain or wrinkle or any other blemish, but holy and blameless.

It is in these words that the husband is to find his personal value to his wife. She has been given an intrinsic value because she is God's daughter and you are her leader but you must receive your external value of her by not considering her current estate but by considering that estate God has tasked you to bring her about to, that external value you crave in a wife.

<u>She is Weaker</u>:

(asthenesterō) lit: not strong), (a) weak (physically, or morally), (b) infirm, sick.

Understand that she has personal issues because she is weaker; she feels things in a more intense way than you do. Her fear of things naturally overwhelm her, if a mouse can make her climb on top of a table how much more do you think her fear of you will cause her to react erratically? She is more prone to depression[38]. A study undertaken by The University of Cambridge has revealed that women are the more empathetic sex, while men are more analytical and logical. In contrast, men follow what is described as a systemizing approach, meaning they analyze the situation and work on a rule-based system. The study suggests these results are in part due to exposure levels to fetal testosterone, and genetic variation.

Weaker refers to physical and emotional weakness, not intellectual inferiority. She is weaker like Eve in the garden who was deceived by Satan when she fell to the lust of the flesh, the lust of the eye, and the pride of life. The Bible doesn't say that Adam was deceived by Satan but that Eve was deceived by Satan.

- 1 Tim. 2:14 And Adam was not the one deceived; it was the woman who was deceived and became a sinner.

> The woman is 'weaker' because she is more prone to deception and she feels more intensely.

In this sense the woman is 'weaker' because she is more prone to deception and she feels more intensely. Women are five times more likely to cry and when startled their response is to scream. They feel your displeasure more intensely and deny fault at any cost. Every spouse has, to some degree, been deceived by the lies of modern feminism because feminism's message draws on the woman's desire to be more empowering, as it says in Genesis, to rule over her husband. Understand that your spouse 'intensely feels' that desire even when she doesn't know she does. Have your spouse ever said to you "I don't know why I did that", it is because there are some things deep inside of her that she doesn't understand. But you as her leader are responsible to understand why she does things even she doesn't understand.

Even though she is subject to deception so are you but to a lesser degree.

- 2 Cor. 11:3 But I am afraid that just as Eve was deceived by the serpent's cunning, your minds may somehow be led astray from your sincere and pure devotion to Christ.

In one context, "weaker vessel" likely carries the idea of "worth protecting" as "something to cherish". A boxer who knows he has a weak abdomen lowers his hands to protect it or if he has experienced a hard liver punch he responds by moving his stance to the right of his opponent to protect his liver against his enemy's punch. In the same way the husband protects his wife as if she is a weaker part of himself.

- Gen. 2:23-24 The man said, "This is now bone of my bones

and flesh of my flesh; she shall be called 'woman,' for she was taken out of man." 24That is why a man leaves his father and mother and is united to his wife, and they become one flesh.

- Eph. 5:28-29 In this same way, husbands ought to love their wives as their own bodies. He who loves his wife loves himself. 29After all, no one ever hated their own body, but they feed and care for their body, just as Christ does the church—

God lets you know ahead of time that if you have a wife she will be problematic and He expects for you, in the midst of those problems, to feed and care for her.

Now we as farmers have fields that have been infected with weeds (modern feminism) and that coupled with the Genesis curse of our desiring to dominate each other has exasperated the problem. Now this desire of ours to dominate her is Satanic especially since we have been tasked to care for our weaker vessels; which is Christ-like. For when we act as those who are without understanding, as those who are without knowledge, after we marry them we take it for granted that they are wives but to our displeasure we find out that they are only spouses, then what? When they don't act like wives we resent them and since as modern feminists any resentment of them establishes their fear of patriarchy which then leads to divorce.

Feminism was like a left jab thrown to hid the impending devastating right cross of modern feminism. You don't see it coming but (boom) when it hits it is like the storm/torrent of Luke 6 that devastates your marriage, we will investigate this passage a little later on.

<u>They are Heirs with You of the Grace of Life</u>

When Christ died on the cross for you He did for your spouse also. He made you both joint heirs under Him of all that God as His Father owns. Not only has God adopted your spouse to share in

Christ's inheritance (as He is the only begotten Son of God) He has also given her eternal life and He has given her eternal life not based on how good of a wife she has been to you but out of His grace He has extended eternal life to her.

Back in Genesis when she sinned and enticed her husband to sin along with her she died, that is she was separated from God, and then she hid from God along with Adam. But God out of His grace went looking for her and finding her naked, (that is uncovered by His glory because of her sin) He covered her with the skins of a Lamb. Now she had done nothing to deserve this covering but God extended His grace to her and covered her with what was a depiction of the blood of Christ seen in the skins of a lamb slain to provide that covering of her sins.

- John 1:29 The next day John saw Jesus coming toward him and said, "Look, the Lamb of God, who takes away the sin of the world!
- Rev. 13:8 All inhabitants of the Earth will worship the beast—all whose names have not been written in the Lamb's book of life, the Lamb who was slain from the creation of the world.

Now since Christ died on the cross for her, and adopted her as His daughter, and shared Christ's inheritance with her, and gave her eternal life, which means He has brought her into an eternal relationship with Him. Since God values her so much you would think you would also, I mean at least out of respect for God.

Since Christ suffered so much for her do you think you should be willing as her husband and leader to suffer just a little bit? After all she is the 'weaker vessel'. A chain is as strong as its weakest link, if you don't manage the stress placed on that link then the chain, and your marriage will surely break.

As Eve stood before God with inadequate fig leaves to cover her nakedness she stands before you clothed in those same fig leaves. And as

God showed mercy and grace to her by covering her nakedness with the skins of the Lamb you also should show a little mercy and grace. Now if you can't, if you are saying she has hurt me too much, my wounds are too deep, all I want to do is get away I understand but you must also understand that when you don't extend mercy and grace to your spouse your prayers to God will be hindered when you ask Him to extend mercy and grace to you.

<u>So That Your Prayers May Not Be Hindered</u>

Prayers in 1 Peter 3:7 may refer to all of your prayers, this is not out of the question but for sure in context it refers to all the prayers where you ask Him to turn your spouse into a wife. Are you tired of praying to God to do something about your spouse's attitude and she still remains the same? Are you tired of pouring out your heart to God, have you warned Him that you have reached the end of your rope and you can't take it anymore? Does it seem like the more you fall on your knees the worse she gets? Maybe you should ask God why He doesn't hear your cry. If you do He is telling you right now to read the last phrase of 1 Peter 3:7, your prayers are hindered because you are not doing the first 2 phrases of 1 Peter 3:7 to 'live with your wives in an understanding way' and 'show honor to the woman as the weaker vessel'.

> How can you trust God's power when you don't trust His word?

Prayer like faith is dead without works. How can you trust God's power when you don't trust His word? For all of you who have given up on your marriages God asks you a question He expects you to answer, it is this; Why do you call me Lord and do not what I say?

- Luke 6:46 "Why do you call me, 'Lord, Lord,' and do not do what I say? 47 As for everyone who comes to me and hears my words and puts them into practice, I will show you what they are like. 48 They are like a man building a house, who dug down deep and laid the foundation on rock. When a flood came, the torrent struck that house but could not shake it, because it was well built. 49But the one who hears my words and does not put them into practice is like a man who built a house on the ground without a foundation. The moment the torrent struck that house, it collapsed and its destruction was complete."

Let's pick apart what God is saying. If He is your Lord then by definition you obey Him, but you are not obeying Him so why do you call Him Lord? God is confused that you call Him Lord and emphasize calling Him your Lord (by repeating twice that He is your Lord) when you don't do what He is saying, first answer that question.

Now the next part of the verse is for you who are slow of learning. God gives you an example to follow. The smart builder of a home or marriage builds his marriage on a firm foundation (the Word of God) but the foolish builder of a home or a marriage builds his marriage on sand (a pretty face, and a firm butt and tits). So now God asks you what did you build your home/marriage on? He doesn't expect you to answer because the storm has come. Note that the verse doesn't say (if) the storm comes but (when) it comes. The devastating storm (torrent) comes to every marriage, both good and bad but the husband who practices the Word of God his marriage will survive the storm. But the foolish husband who doesn't practice God's Word this same storm that the wise husband's marriage survived will destroy the foolish husband's marriage.

Feminism was a right jab used to distract you from seeing modern feminism's hard gut-punch and debilitating liver punch to your marriage. Taken together both feminism and modern feminism has led to the paradigm shift we are experiencing in marriages. But all is not lost, God sees your predicament and has made a way for you to experience the love He had in mind for you to experience in your marriage.

CHAPTER FIVE

(The Implementation)

<u>Your Marriage is a Metastasizing Cancer</u>

Don't treat her harshly when she proves not to be the perfect wife you foolishly expected but instead cleanse her with the Word of God. Remember just as the curse was not one sided, you both desire to dominate each other, neither is the implementation of the solution one sided, you must both submit to each other (Eph. 5:21).

Have your prayers gone unanswered and your efforts at reconciliation been rebuffed? Has the discord you are experiencing in your marriage reduced you to hopelessness? Are you ready to give up but the cost of child-support and alimony give you pause? Have you come to the conclusion that you made a bad choice and are unable to bear the burden? Are you like the man who is rebuffed for wearing his wedding ring on the wrong hand who then retorts "I wear my wedding ring on the wrong hand because I married the wrong woman!" Caught between a rock and a hard place; staying with her is too unpleasant but divorcing her is too costly. God has a word for you.

- Eph. 5:25 Husbands, love your wives, just as Christ loved the church and gave himself up for her 26to make her holy, cleansing her by the washing with water through the word, 27and to present her to himself as a radiant church, without stain or wrinkle or any other blemish, but holy and blameless.]

Though we are under the Genesis curse which has been exasperated by modern feminism all is not hopeless for as we obey God's instructions concerning marriage we can mitigate the effects of the curse and restrict the metastasis of modern feminism throughout our whole marriage. How so, first let us gain hope from Christ's example of

His bad marriage that went wrong. In Ephesians 1:4 Jesus' purpose of selecting the church (His bride) was so that Christ would have a wife that He could present to Himself in all her perfection.

- Eph. 1:4a 'For he chose us in him before the creation of the world to be holy and blameless in his sight...'

I know you don't see any perfection in your spouse but God did create the woman for the man, feminism has taught her that she is a person in and of herself, that she don't need no man she need only to be strong and independent. But just as the woman is part of the man so the man is part of the woman. She is incomplete without him but sadly she will only come to recognize this truth after she divorces him.

> Your job is to clean up her imperfections so that you can have a wife that is holy and without fault.

<u>Your Job is to Remove the Cancer</u>

No matter how good of a wife you pick she isn't perfect, but now speaking to the ideal as opposed to what is practicable, your job is to clean up her imperfections so that you can have a wife that is holy and without fault. Your job as her husband and her leader doesn't end until she is pleasing in God's sight. Whenever you see a fault your job is not to become disturbed by it and wallow in dissatisfaction but envision what it will take of you to remove the cancer without killing the patient, realizing that she is the weaker of you two.

But you retort, I hear what you are saying but I long ago have given up on effecting anything she does, she is so hard-headed and uncompromising I just as soon keep my mouth shut and stay out of her way. God understands the difficulties you are experiencing with her but he has not left you alone, He says in Matt. 28:20b "And surely I am with you always, to the very end of the age." But now before He says that He says in 18b "All authority in heaven and on Earth has been given to me." When God speaks of your duties as leader He never means apart from His power and authority. If you have been failing in your role as leader it is because you are depending on your own means and methods. God doesn't use your means and methods, they have and will continue to fail for His ways are as high above your ways as the heavens are above the Earth and as far away from you ways as the East is from the West.

In Isaiah 55:11 God proclaims 'so is my word that goes out from my mouth: It will not return to me empty, but will accomplish what I desire and achieve the purpose for which I sent it.' Stop using your means and methods and start using God's Word (His ways) because they come with a promise, 'they will accomplish what He desires, not what you desire and they will achieve God's purpose for your marriage not your purpose. When your desire and purpose for your marriage lines up with God's desire and purpose for it, then you are depending on Him and His power is brought to bear on your marriage. You as a husband will become pleasing to God in all your ways because your ways will be God's ways. When your wife can behold that your ways and God's ways are the same then she will become more submissive to you because she will see no difference between you and God.

<u>What Pleases a Godly Woman? A Godly Man</u>

Her job is not to please you but to please God and by that you should be pleased too. If she understands that you want her to be pleasing to God and not you then she will become more submissive to you because she will equate submission to your will as submission to the will of God because both wills will be the same thing. She will seek to please you because she will know that in pleasing you she will be pleasing God because both you and God want the same thing for her.

> Her job is not to please you but to please God and by that you should be pleased too.

Marriages run into problems when the husband wants what God doesn't. Have you ascertained if your desires of your wife are in line with God's desires for her? Has she not been submissive to you because you are not submissive to God? Are you really the problem and not her? Unlikely, but what is likely is that neither of you wanted what God wanted for your marriage to begin with, so like in all marriages there is enough blame to spread to the both of you. Now your spouse can play the blame game because God didn't make her the leader of your marriage, He made you the leader therefore you can't blame her even if she has, practically speaking, usurped the authority in your home. God doesn't look to her as leader neither does He reward her leadership because God made you the leader and therefore He made you responsible to manage your marriage, and turn your spouse into the wife God wants her to be.

You have become a detestable sight to God and to your spouse when you allow her to wear your pants. Remember how weak and feckless Adam looked as he just stood by Eve as she took control over the situation speaking to Satan and handing Adam the forbidden fruit to eat. Also remember the devastation that resulted from Eve's leadership, is there any resemblance to the devastation you see in your marriage? God has given you the leadership role ideally, positionally and practically and as such your job is to cleanse you spouse until she turns into a wife.

> You have become a detestable sight to God and to your spouse when you allow her to wear your pants.

Heat rises, babies cry, and leadership will be challenged until challenge becomes futile. Come what may your leadership must become non-negotiable.

Husbands can't cleanse their wives in the exact manner as Christ cleansed His bride the church through removing every sin and imparting to her His righteousness. But husbands can seek to imitate Christ's cleansing of his wife through encouraging her to live according to God's instruction for wives. In order to cleanse your wife and present her to yourself as having not spot or wrinkle you must imitate Christ as He cleansed His bride. So what did He do? He placed her benefit above His own and if you don't place her benefit above your own then you can't cleanse your wife.

- Eph. 5:25 Husbands, love your wives, just as Christ loved the church and gave himself up for her.

So what does it mean to place her benefit above your own? It doesn't mean give her everything she wants but give her everything she needs to become a wife and a daughter of God and a spiritual maturing woman. If that means you must study the bible more to lead her in the truths of the bible then so be it. If that means you must limit your employment to 40 hours a week so you can spend more time at home leading the family then so be it. If the means you drive the older car so she can drive the nicer one then so be it. If that means you only have one car note or just one car so that she can stay at home then so be it. If for her to fully fulfill her innate desires to nurture her family you have to downsize your house so she doesn't have to work outside her home, then so be it. The bible uses the word 'edification[39]' and this must be your mindset when it comes to your wife.

<u>Care for your Wife as if you are Caring for Yourself!</u>

I know this attitude cuts across your grain, isn't she supposed to obey you as her lord, didn't Abraham's wife Sarah address Abraham as her lord, isn't she supposed to serve you as her leader, wouldn't everything work out if she just stood in her place; beneath you? That attitude is demonic, you will have to get rid of it if you are to have a successful marriage. Now listen carefully to the appropriate attitude you are to have for your wife. Husbands consider your wife as part of yourselves.

- Eph. 5:29 After all, no one ever hated their own body, but they feed and care for their body, just as Christ does the church— 30for we are members of his body. 31"For this reason a man will leave his father and mother and be united to his wife, and the two will become one flesh." 32This is a profound mystery—but I am talking about Christ and the church. 33However, each one of you also must love his wife as he loves himself, and the wife must respect her husband.

To be impatient, uncaring, and selfish towards her is to be impatient, uncaring and denying of your own self.

To treat your own wife harshly is to hate your own body, to be impatient, uncaring, and selfish towards her is to be impatient, uncaring and denying of your own self. To spite her is to strike your own face, to harm her is to harm yourself and not to care for her is to take a stand against God who will take a stand against you by cutting off your prayers in retaliation. A man who tears down his own wife must live with the destruction he caused to his own self. God never advises you to punish your wife but just the opposite to build her up in the Lord. In this way you will show love for your own self, making your home one of peace and contentment.

Now in the fifth chapter of Ephesians God has a lot to say to you so listen carefully.

<u>That Awful Word Submission</u>

- Eph. 5:22 Wives, submit yourselves to your own husbands as you do to the Lord.

Verse 21 instructs husbands and wives to submit to each other this verse acts as a hinge between the preceding verses that deal with wisdom and living under the influence of the Holy Spirit, and the following verses, which consider the relationships between husbands and wives and Christ and the church. In 5:21, Paul says that the one who is filled with the Spirit not only reflects God's goodness in speech and attitudes but also manifests it in willingness to submit to others out of reverence for Christ.

Submission often has unpleasant implications for modern Christian women, perhaps because this principle has been abused in the past and has been used to justify overbearing and self-serving behavior of the husband. But Jesus was willing to submit to the will of his Father and to the agonies of the cross. "Submission" is not a bad word. How do you respond to the idea of submitting to others? Are you willing to place the interests and desires of others ahead of your own in Jesus' name?[40]

Using context to determine just what the bible means when it says submit to one another out of reverence for Christ. Let's consider some of the preceding phrases:

- 8For you were once darkness, but now you are light in the Lord. Live as children of light

- 11Have nothing to do with the fruitless deeds of darkness, but rather expose them.
- 15Be very careful, then, how you live—not as unwise but as wise, 16making the most of every opportunity, because the days are evil. 17Therefore do not be foolish, but understand what the Lord's will is.
- 18b ...Instead, be filled with the Spirit,
- 20 always giving thanks to God the Father for everything, in the name of our Lord Jesus Christ.

By submitting to each other both husband and wife live as children of light. Reject your old foolish ways of seeking to dominate each other but live according to God's wisdom understanding what God's will for your marriage is; that through depending on the Holy Spirit you both submit to the good of each other.

- 22 For wives, this means submit to your husbands as to the Lord. 23For a husband is the head of his wife as Christ is the head of the church. He is the Savior of his body, the church. 24As the church submits to Christ, so you wives should submit to your husbands in everything.

> By submitting to each other both husband and wife live as children of light.

The Bible does not require wives to be slaves for their husbands—that is not what the Bible means by "submission." The wife should submit to the husband's authority, but the Christian husband must use his authority with consideration and respect for his wife. He must not be a tyrant, faithless, unloving, or impatient. Likewise, the wife should not be rebellious, subversive, or contradicting. Inherent in the Greek word submission (hypotássō) is the idea that one is properly "under God's arrangement," i.e. submitting to the Lord (His plan for your marriage).

The problem with marriages in our modern culture today is that they don't follow God's order/arrangement. Feminism has struck out in the opposite direction God has set marriages to prosper from. As is evident by our culture today going opposite to God's design leads to failure and the greater the rejection of His order the greater the destruction of marriage. The word submission is anathema to feminism and yet it is God's order that leads to successful, joyful, and fulfilled marriages.

<u>Love, Honor and Obey?</u>

"I don't think so!" said the blushing bride. Most brides today will not object to the word Love being used in their wedding vows as long as no details are attached but to a lesser degree some would agree with using the word Honor as long as details are attached but hardly any at all would agree with the word Obey with or without any details.

Even for the feminist let alone the modern feminist words like submission, obedience, and headship are fighting words. But just what does it mean when God says that husbands must be the head of their wives? If feminists understood the burden that puts on husbands and the blessings of God that accrues for the wife they would have a whole different attitude towards submission, obedience, and headship.

Ephesians 5:21-33 explains:

- 21Submit to one another out of reverence for Christ.

> Women would be more accepting of male leadership if the men were more caring of the woman's needs and men would be more caring of the woman's needs if women were more cooperative.

The benefit of submission is <u>one sided</u>, the husband must submit to his wife for her benefit, that is that her needs be met, and the wife must submit to her husband, <u>also</u> for her benefit because everything her husband says and does is for her benefit first and foremost. This is the relationship between husbands and wives God has established. Now the reason why so many women including feminist object to the idea of submission, leadership, and headship is because so many husbands don't fulfill the design of husbandry God established. Women would be more accepting of male leadership if the men were more caring of the woman's needs and men would be more caring of the woman's needs if women were more cooperative. What can be said except until both set their pride aside neither will experience the peace and harmony God intended marriage to promote.

- 22Wives, submit yourselves to your own husbands as you do to the Lord. 23For the husband is the head of the wife as Christ is the head of the church, his body, of which he is the Savior. 24Now as the church submits to Christ, so also wives should submit to their husbands in everything.

Verses 22-24 is probably the most hated verses in the Bible for our modern, western, feminist culture. For the wife to obey her husband as if he is God causes the hair on the back of their necks to stand up straight. But why would God command such a thing of wives? It seems so impractical especially for a woman who has been raised not to trust men and men who have shown a propensity to misuse women. Well God has anticipated the push-back and given His reason for the command, He introduces His reason with the word 'For'. 'For' means 'because', in the same way Christ is the leader or head of the church, and He is the Savior of His body, the church, because of that the wife should obey her husband in the same manner as if he were God. I know you hear what the Bible says but don't understand what it means. As Christ gave Himself to be the savior of the church, you husbands must give of yourself to save your wife. So then how is it that the husband saves his wife?

The idea here is that as Christ gave himself to save his bride, the church; as he practiced self-denial and made her an object of intense care to preserve her, so ought the husband to manifest a similar care to save his wife from want, affliction, pain, and herself. He ought to regard himself as her natural protector, anticipating and providing for her needs; as under obligation to comfort her in her trial, even as Christ does the church. What a beautiful illustration of the spirit a husband should manifest. The care which Christ has shown for his "bride," the church the husband must show for his wife!

> She never should have married you, you are not fit to be her husband if she doesn't see Christ in you.

But now I hear many of your wives complain that you are no savior, this is to your shame as her husband. She never should have married you, you are not fit to be her husband if she doesn't see Christ in you.

So what does it mean for husbands to be the head of their wives, it means that husbands must love them.

- 25 Husbands love your wives, just as Christ loved the church.

> He gave up his life for her 26to make her holy and clean, washed by the cleansing of God's word. 27He did this to present her to himself as a glorious church without a spot or wrinkle or any other blemish. Instead, she will be holy and without fault.

- 33However, each one of you also must love his wife as he loves himself, and the wife must respect her husband.

If you want any hope of your spouse cooperating and following your Christian leadership, if you want her to recognize that you are the head of the family then you must love her. Love is not an emotion but a verb, it indicates action, and can be seen in what is done. When your love becomes visible to your spouse, she will be more willing to follow your leadership because you put her welfare first among your list of considerations.

But what exactly is Love? Do I convey my love for her by appreciating the things she does for me? Do I convey my love for her by making her 'happy'? Do I convey my love for her by being affectionate with her? No, none of these things will convey the Love God requires you to have for your wife. Then what is love? Love is sacrifice! You show the type of love God commands of you to have for your wife by sacrificing for her.

- John 3:16 For God so loved the world that he gave his one and only Son, that whoever believes in him shall not perish but have eternal life.

Again Christ gives us the example;

- 25 Husbands love your wives, just as Christ loved the church. He gave up his life for her 26to make her holy and clean, washed by the cleansing of God's word.

You sacrifice yourself, not to make her happy, but you do the things that make her holy, and clean so that she might become perfect for you. This is the transaction of a godly marriage; she gets everything she needs to become a godly woman and you get a wife who is without spot or wrinkle or any other blemish.

Once you love your wife in this manner then the duty of the wife becomes submission to their husbands in the Lord, which includes honoring and obeying him, from the principle that he always does for her what develops her spiritually maturity so that she resembles a daughter of God. The duty of husbands is to love their wives. The love of Christ for the church is the example, which is constant in spite of her failures, inadequacies, and unattractive proclivities.

If the modern feminist woman knew God's plan to bless her through her husband she would see the foolishness of rejecting his leadership. There was a time when a woman received a husband was considered a time of great joy and praise to God. But that time has changed for the modern woman because your dole as her husband has changed. There was a time when a man refused to let his wife work, he was the provider and she appreciated and respected his leadership but now you have changed insisting your wife works because the culture insists that you have a certain level of creature comforts. You pay too heavy of a price and she has to carry too heavy a load. That time of her blessing God for your husbandry can be restored through a cleansing by the Word of God for you both.

> If the modern woman knew God's plan to bless her through her husband she would see the foolishness of her rejecting his leadership.

It is through the Word that your spouse can be turned into a wife and you into a husband. Of the two Greek words translated "word" in the bible the one here in

Ephesians is that which signifies not "the word" existing as a definite thought in the mind, but "the word" as audibly spoken. In Greek, the original language of the New Testament, two different Greek words are used to refer to the word of God? One is logos, and the other is rhema. In Strong's Concordance #3056 (lógos) is a broad term meaning "reasoning expressed by words." Rhema carries the idea of speaking the word and can carry the idea of speaking the word in conversation as understood in 2 Tim. 3:16-17. So then in Ephesians 5:26 Rhema is used to connote conversation as differing from Logos which would be used to connote logic or reason. Cleanse your wife (remove every spot and wrinkle) by holding an informal bible study with her in everyday conversation speaking to her out of the wisdom (logos) of the word.

- 2 Timothy 3:16-17 'All Scripture is <u>God-breathed</u> and is useful for teaching, rebuking, correcting and training in righteousness, 17so that the servant of God may be thoroughly equipped for every good work.'

My Pastor related a conversation he had with his wife where he killed three wasps' nests that set up residence on his front porch. He decided to take advantage of the situation by turning to his wife and asking "since God has a purpose for everything he creates what do you think was God's purpose for creating wasps?" He turned the conversation from killing wasp nests (God's purpose of a husband's role; protection) to the building of nests (God's purpose of a woman's role; making a home). That conversation could expand into how the man can do the things she is uncomfortable with and the things she can do that he is horrible at. Then discuss the wisdom of following God's purpose for your marriage and the benefits each of you experience when you both fall in line with His model for marriage. Any situation can be turned into a conversation in which the word of God (rhema) can prosper and your wife can be cleansed.

Inform you spouse that you are going to bake a cake and you want her advice; you want to use a sugar substitute instead of using real sugar. When she tells you just how stupid your idea is ask her why the ingredient sugar is so important to baking a cake? When she explains that your cake will not be sweet without real sugar explain to her so is our marriage if we continue to stop being sweet to each other.

Ask her why one of her friends dropped out of college. Then ask your spouse if her friend lacked commitment to obtaining her collegiate goals? Then traverse to the truth that anything worth achieving, like a college degree, is worth committing to like our marriage. We will only benefit from it if we both are committed to it. All marriages encounter difficulties, it is in the midst of traversing those difficulties that we must remain committed to our marriage or else we will drop out of it like her friend dropped out of college, except our family will suffer infinitely more. Discuss the benefits of your marriage and why God hates divorce. Re-emphasize your commitment to endure all the difficulties of marriage as long as she allows you to be a godly husband and not being a godly husband is a line you will not cross. The next day ask her "Honey, what is a godly husband?"

These conversations need not be forced, if you look for the opportunities these types of marriage issues will present themselves. Dr. Tony Evans, my homiletics professor at seminary, is a master of illustrating his sermon messages. He was asked where did all of his illustrations come from, he answered 'everyday life'.

Back in 1867 Daniel Jacobs' son Erasmus use to play by picking up shinny stones along the river Orange to throw. These stones had laid at everyone's feet going un-noticed until one day his mother took notice of them and that was the start of the 'De Beers Diamond Company of South Africa'. In the same manner everyday precious gems lay just at your feet if you recognize them you can use them in the cleansing aspect that is necessary to turn your spouse into a wife.

These types of conversations with your spouse need not be long theological discourses remembering that the average attention span of a human being is only 8.25 seconds. This is down from 12 seconds in the year 2000. There is evidence to suggest that excessive use of social media can have a negative impact on our attention spans. On the other hand, if we are engaged in something that we find interesting or enjoyable, we may be able to maintain our focus for much longer than usual.[41]

Don't make God's instruction boring or uninteresting for it is neither, it is powerful and can make sense to your spouse where you can't.

- Heb. 4:12 For the word of God is living and active, and sharper than any two-edged sword, penetrating even as far as the division of soul and spirit, and of joints and marrows, and able to judge the thoughts and intentions of the heart.

Just as Christ gave Himself to cleanse the church to make her without stain or wrinkle or any other blemish so also the husband must give of himself to make his wife clean and holy, without stain or wrinkle or blemish. The husband who grounds his spouse and their relationship in the Word of God will honor (to ascribe value to) her and thereby present to himself a wife without spot, wrinkle or blemish.

<u>Pride is the Problem in All Marriages Gone Bad</u>

Feminism is entitlement, the root of which is pride, the foundation of all your marriage problems.

- 1 Jn. 2:16 For everything in the world—the lust of the flesh, the lust of the eyes, and the pride of life—comes not from the Father but from the world.
- Prov. 6:17 -19 16These six things the Lord hates, Yes, seven are an abomination to Him: 17A proud look, A lying tongue,

Hands that shed innocent blood, 18A heart that devises wicked plans, Feet that are swift in running to evil, 19A false witness who speaks lies, And one who sows discord among brethren.

> Feminism is entitlement, the root of which is pride, the foundation of all your marriage problems.

When your wife corrects you for something you know you should not have done and you out of pride responded defensively, correct yourself through a conversation that asks her the question, "honey of the seven things God hates the most which of them does He place first on His list and why?" This followed by a definition of pride and a request for her to help you see when Satan motivates you out of pride will help her see it when she is also acting out of pride or at least will cause her to be less defensive to the correction you are seeking.

To women raised in our culture accepting blame is anathema but it is much more palatable when the correction comes from the mouth of God than from your mouth. And since you know she has a problem with accepting blame as best you can help her to see the truth without her having to admit to the fault.

> To women raised in our culture accepting blame is anathema.

Communication is best had when fault is not addressed openly. Women love attention and praise so lavish it upon her when she fulfills her role as wife, rather than proclaiming her faults when she doesn't. Praise her when she allows you to make a decision then inform her how the intent of your decision was to her benefit. Then expand the conversation to include how your love for her drives you to always do those things that benefit her first, the family second and you last. Ask her if there is some decision you made that she didn't agree with then explain to her why you made that decision and the benefits it brings to her. Discuss with her what she thinks you should have done and then explain to her why you didn't. But if her idea was a better idea then thank her and commit to considering her better idea in the future.

<u>Your Wife's Ungodly Friends: The Sisterhood</u>

The wise husband goes out of your way to insure his wife has godly women friends and interrupts as much as possible her friendships with ungodly women because she is sure to imitate the friends she has. Many a marriage has been ruined by advice from the council of the 'sisterhood'; ungodly female friends. There was a time, before the 1960s when women understood that marriage meant commitment and if a young wife spoke of breaking up her marriage she would be chastised by her community of women. They would tell her to take her little fast as* back to her husband and work things out. But that community is long gone, now she goes to the 'sisterhood' or social media where they echo back to her what she wants to hear. Things like 'you deserve to be happy' 'you need to live your full life' 'you deserve better' 'you got married too young' 'divorce isn't a bad thing, at least you get alimony and child support', 'you're not his slave or his mother, he needs to grow up'.

It is in the nature of women to be repulsed at the thought that maybe she was the one to be at fault for her troubled marriage. This coupled with the fact that in their nature is the need to be viewed as the victim in all situations. They have a need for sympathy and attention from others. Beware if she is seeking sympathy and attention from other men because it will not be long before she seeks sexual pleasure from him also. You see in a woman's feelings resides the flaw that she is never the problem, in her mind you are always the problem and after she has done everything right for the marriage and you in your masculinity rejected all her righteous efforts at being the perfect wife for you the marriage failed. She will tell her friends "I gave up so much for him and this marriage but he just didn't appreciate anything I did for him. I just don't know what to do, I'm thinking it may be the best for the both of us if we separate." To which her 'echo chamber' the sisterhood will not only agree but encourage her to. She is not aware and it should be brought to her attention that the women who make up her immediate group of the 'sisterhood' are not married, lonely, wish they had a man and will be looking to get with her husband as soon as they talk her into opening the door, through divorce, to you. Keep this mantra in mind 'single women keep women single'.

It is because of their need to be right and viewed as the victim in all situations that women seek friends that will be their 'echo chamber'. Now an 'echo chamber' is an environment where a person only encounters information or opinions that reflect and reinforce their own. The reason why your spouse doesn't have godly friends is because they will reject her leaving God's path for a godly wife to walk and disagree with her detouring from that path. Her ungodly friends will echo back to her, her opinion that she is perfect and you have victimized her.

You see feminism always defends the 'sisterhood'. The motto of the 'sisterhood' is women are always right, good, and perfect. Women are progressive and men are regressive. Now the sisterhood is strong and bends to their will any detractors. Know that your battle is not just with your spouse but it is also with the sisterhood. You are just one voice but the sisterhood has a chorus of voices, they are the Mass Choir all singing in harmony the same lies of feminism. Naturally your spouse will be unduly influenced by them. Part of your battle with your spouse is to limit her exposure to the sisterhood.

> Know that your battle is not just with your spouse but it is also with the sisterhood.

Though the sisterhood are many 'one with God is a majority'. God defends His leaders with whom He is well pleased. Refer to Numbers chapter 12 to read about God spitting in the face of Moses sister Miriam because she challenged Moses leadership.

- Num. 12:1 Miriam and Aaron began to talk against Moses because of his Cushite wife, for he had married a Cushite. 2"Has the Lord spoken only through Moses?" they asked. "Hasn't he also spoken through us?" And the Lord heard this.
- 9The anger of the Lord burned against them, and he left them. 10When the cloud lifted from above the tent, Miriam's skin was leprous...
- 14a The Lord replied to Moses, "If her father had spit in her face, would she not have been in disgrace for seven days?...

Beware if your unhappy spouse is spending a lot of time on social media because some social media have algorithms that are designed to show users content that aligns with their interests and beliefs, in other words they become her 'echo chamber' also.

If your marriage is going off rail then see to it that you introduce into your spouse's orbit godly women and above all introduce her to the best friend she can possibly have, Jesus Christ.

- Proverbs 14:24 One who has unreliable friends soon comes to ruin, but there is a friend who sticks closer than a brother.

That friend that sticks closer than a brother is Jesus Christ, the Word of God.

- John 1:14 The Word became flesh and made his dwelling among us. We have seen his glory, the glory of the one and only Son, who came from the Father, full of grace and truth.

<u>You Chose This Unclean Woman, You Have to Clean Her Up!</u>

"Why would I clean this old one up when I can get a new younger model?" I'm sure you have heard the saying, 'out of the frying pan into the fire'. First marriages still end in divorce at a rate of approximately 35-50%, while second marriages face an even higher likelihood of dissolution, ranging from 60-70% or more. This significant increase in the likelihood of divorce in second marriages can be attributed to various factors, including blended family dynamics, lingering emotional baggage from previous relationships, and the pressures of adjusting to a new partner's lifestyle.[42]

> You Chose This Unclean Woman, You Have to Clean Her Up!

But now some of you have chosen a spouse that has stuffed her ears so that she can't hear your pleas or the Word of God. What then? Pray, pray and then pray some more! Let her see you fall down on your knees and let her hear your prayers to God for a family that He will be pleased with. Continue to invite her to pray with you, if she continually refuses then pray for her salvation first.

Understand that a spouse will reject the truth to escape her responsibility. She will turn a deaf ear to you because she can't stand the idea of you being right and she being at fault. Even though you chose her against the advice of God's Word, God still holds you responsible to clean her up.

- 2 Corinthians 6:14 Be ye not unequally yoked together with unbelievers: for what fellowship hath righteousness with unrighteousness? and what communion hath light with darkness? 14 Do not be unequally yoked with unbelievers.

A yoke is a wooden bar that joins two oxen together to a plow they must pull. An "unequally yoked" team has one stronger ox and one weaker. The weaker ox would walk more slowly than the stronger one, causing the load to go around in circles. When oxen are unequally yoked, they cannot perform the task set before them. Instead of working together, they are at odds with one another. Their marriage goes around in circles not accomplishing anything.

If you have a spouse not receptive to God's word you have made your choice, you have your burden to bear—for God hates divorce! What do you do when your spouse has heard her fill of the Word of God and has taken your kindness to her as a weakness and she feels she can do better than you on the dating market?[43]

Your situation is not uncommon to men, you will still need a miracle from God to turn your spouse into a wife so pray to God as you live righteously before Him and your spouse.

- Jeremiah 32:27 "'I am the Lord, the God of all mankind. Is anything too hard for me?
- James 5:16b '...The prayer of a righteous person is powerful and effective.'

A Word about Prayer

I have been saved for quite a while now, 48 years of adult life to be exact and as I take account of my prayers I see that the vast majority of the time I request something from God He has told me "no ", not later but "no". Is that your experience, why is that? Well I may not be as spiritual as you but for me James 4:2b-3 speaks volumes about me.

- ...You do not have because you do not ask God. 3When you ask, you do not receive, because you ask with wrong motives, that you may spend what you get on your pleasures.

> We have a back-end God but God wants to be a front-loaded God.

I miss a lot of the God's blessings because I don't ask Him for them. I don't ask Him because the things God wants for me I don't want for myself. Like Samson I saw a 'Delilah' and told my Father "get her for me", but the good wife God brought into my presence I ignored. God brought before me a good wife but I didn't want her, I wanted the 'Delilah' that caught my eye. Isn't that truly the reason why your marriage is a mess? And then you pray to God with the most fervor after all of your attempts have failed, it looks like this; I complain to my spouse, and when she doesn't respond I sulk and become moody, I whine and then I give up and call on God to do something with 'the woman He has given me'. I depend on God to be my Calvary arriving just in the nick of time. It sounds like this; 'Well I've done all I can do so it's up to you now God. We have a back-end God but God wants to be a front-loaded God. Oh if we had called on Him at the front-end of dating then we wouldn't have to plead with Him on the back-end of a broken marriage. Here is a good prayer we all should petition God for; 'Father, make me want the things you want!'

> "Father, make me want the things you want!"

There are two types of prayers, one I call 'walking prayers' and the second I call 'closet prayers'. Now walking prayers are when you pray without ceasing (1 Thess. 5:17) Strong's Concordance defines 'without ceasing' properly as; nothing left between, i.e. without any unnecessary interval (time-gap). When I pray without ceasing I live my life in a mental state where I'm always in contact with God conversing with Him, being joyful, praising and thanking Him for whatever situation I find myself in.

- 1 Thess. 5:16-18 Always be joyful. 17Never stop praying. 18Be thankful in all circumstances, for this is God's will for you who belong to Christ Jesus.

For I realize that whatever my situation is Rom. 8:28-29 applies:

- 28And we know that <u>God causes everything to work together for the good</u> of those who love God and are called according to his purpose for them. 29For God knew his people in advance, and he chose them <u>to become like his Son,</u> so that his Son would be the firstborn among many brothers and sisters.

I'm joyful, praising and thankful to God because whatever God is allowing to happen to me He is allowing it to happen because His purpose is that my situation conforms me into the image of Jesus Christ. To pray without ceasing is like breathing, it should be a sub-routine that is always running in the back of your mind no matter what else you are doing.

You do know that prayer is so much more than just asking God for stuff. When you are of such a mind-set that the joy, thanks, and praise of God is running in your consciousness as a sub-routine God spontaneously holds out His hand to you with a blessing in it you didn't know was coming or didn't even ask Him for.

As you walk with God meditate in your mind and heart the words of the hymn: 'Order My Steps In Your Word Dear Lord', the first stanza is as follows but the whole hymn is profitable for spiritual growth.

"Order my steps in Your word dear Lord, Lead me, guide me everyday, Send Your anointing, Father I pray, Order my steps in Your word, Please, order my steps in Your word"

Then there are 'closet prayers' spoken of in Matt. 6:6.

- But thou, when thou prayest, enter into thy closet, and when thou hast shut thy door, pray to thy Father which is in secret; and thy Father which seeth in secret shall reward thee openly. (KJV)

Now closet prayers function under a different order than walking prayers. The acronym P.R.A.Y. is helpful;

P: <u>P</u>raise God

R: <u>R</u>epent of your sins

A: <u>P</u>ray for another

Y: then pray for <u>Y</u>ourself

Closet prayers make requests of God but those requests are preceded by praise, repentance, and praying for others then expressing your requests. But you must be mindful that the sole purpose of your requests are not because you want to indulge in some personal pleasure. If you pray to hit the lottery even if you promise to tithe 50% of it to God He probably will not honor your request because in actuality all you want to do is purchase stuff for yourself.

If you ask God to strengthen you to be the leader your spouse needs you to be so that she will cook you meals and give you sex when you want it, God probably will not answer your prayer in the affirmative. But if you ask God to strengthen you to be the leader that brings Him glory and edifies your wife then you stand much more of a chance of God answering you request in the affirmative. If you ask God to help you set your pride aside or give you patience as you deal with your spouse's infirmities, or ask Him to give you an understanding of your spouse's inner motivations so that you can deal with her in a godly manner then most likely God will answer your request in the affirmative.

If you are looking for a wife understand that you are not perfect and need a lot of work. That being so here is a prayer you should consider making, "Father, I don't deserve one of your daughters so please I pray that You strengthen me to become the type of husband that will bring honor to You by being the husband your daughter needs and deserves."

> I pray that You strengthen me to become the type of husband that will bring honor to You by being the husband your daughter needs and deserves.'

Now believing that God will do a thing has no bearing on whether He will do it or not. God is not bound by your faith if your faith is not bound on what God has said. When you pray, as much as possible let God's Word be the foundation upon which you make your request, if you do that then you can be sure that God will hear you and do what He said He will do.

- Isaiah 55:11 so is my word that goes out from my mouth: It will not return to me empty, but will accomplish what I desire and achieve the purpose for which I sent it.

God's desire is that your marriage reflect Christ's love for His church and if you give yourself for your spouse and wash her and cleanse her in God's Word that doesn't mean that God will force your spouse to be a wife. God doesn't force people apart from their will. In the end of all your efforts your spouse will still have to make her own decision to become a wife but you will have done all that God requires of you as her husband.

Feminism like sin has had an effect on your spouse but if you be the husband God wants you to be then He just may reduce the effect of that sin in your messed up situation. I don't want you to lose heart but consider that Jesus Christ has been cleansing His bride for approximately 2,000 years and He still has to work on her. If He hasn't given up on her after 2,000 years then how much longer do you think you will have to work on your spouse?

<u>The Feminist Modern Western Woman is Delusional</u>

Women are addicted to marriage, when they divorce you they don't want to be free from marriage, they want to explore opportunities to find someone better than you because they are delusional in their valuation of themselves. They feel they will be a hot commodity on the dating market only to find that the dating market is a disguise for the hook-up culture. She doesn't know it but the dating market is just a place for her to be humped, pumped and then dumped. Social media dating platforms will provide her many suiters but none for marriage. Dating in the modern western culture has turned into just an attempt for men to have one night stands.

Men are no longer interested in getting married because women are no longer committed to being married. When the storm/torrent of married life hits, and difficulties will bring stress to your marriage, men know that the modern feminist woman will leave them the same way they left their previous husbands. Men also are no longer interested in getting married because the majority of marriages end in divorce and once a man goes through a divorce because of the advantage women have under divorce laws men are hesitant to touch that fire again.

Because of the designation 'irreconcilable differences' a legal way of saying 'My husband doesn't make me happy anymore' modern western cultured women are quick to seek a divorce not realizing that happiness is not found on the other side of marriage.

Your spouse's beauty drew you to her in the same manner as your finances drew her to you. Men don't file for divorce because he loses access to his spouse's beauty but swomen file for divorce because through child-support, alimony, and asset distribution she retains your finances.

If your spouse no longer listens to you or the Word of God introduce her to 'Kevin Samuels' and 'Women Hitting the Wall' and

'Pearl Talk' on You Tube, these programs as well as others should adjust her attitude more towards the experience of a divorced women in the western modern culture.[44]

One of the complaints common among women is that their husbands don't communicate with them. This is probably so because the average woman is a master in controlling the conversation. Their attempt to control the conversation is their attempt to control you. In that control Kevin Samuals informs us to be on the watch for the S.I.G.N. language they use. If you are making a point that calls them to take responsibility they will Shame you, Insult you, Guilt trip you, and Need to be right. If you want to lead the conversation then you must not be sidetracked by such tactics. Stay on point because when she starts using S.I.G.N. language she is admitting she has lost the argument.

Use programs like 'Kevin Samuels' and 'Women Hitting the Wall' and 'Pearl Talk' on You Tube to set the parameters of a conversation you wish to have with your spouse. Conversations you would like to have with your spouse like, I don't like the way you speak to me, or you are lacking in respect for my leadership, or the kids don't respect me because you don't, or you are spending too much time with your friends, or I don't care for the people you associate with because they will lead to our divorce, etc.. Stop being afraid to broach significate conversation, ultimately she will respect you for them and when she begins to use S.I.G.N. language just know your positions are prevailing.

Since the modern woman is delusional in her estimation of her own self-worth the older women should have introduced the younger women to the 'female delusion calculator' found on google. Also your spouse should have been introduced to the hell of single mother dating. But if they haven't then you will have to get this information to her. If she is contemplating divorce she will let you know by little things she does and says. The 'female delusion calculator' will help her realize the prize she has in you. Here she will find out just how rare the man she feels is worthy of her actually is. For instance the female delusion calculator reveals:

- Only 0.68 percent of American men are unmarried, 6 feet tall or greater, not obese, between the ages of 30 and 45, and make $80,000+ a year. Explain the percentage to her for the typical woman won't surmise that this is less than one in a hundred.

Then in conversation ask your spouse if that type of man can choose from the top one percent of women in America?[45]

Give her a copy of this work and ask her where she disagrees, this will reveal to her that you understand the things she has been hiding from you. At minimum she should have more respect for you.

<u>She May be Delusional but You Are Still Responsible</u>

It is interesting to note that in Jesus' Earthly ministry He never had a woman not respond to His love for her. Jesus problems always came through the men. Don't be one of those men that your family experiences problems because of your lack of love for them. Love says the hard things in a soft voice.

> Love says the hard things in a soft voice.

Ephesians places the responsibility for a marriage on the husband and if you did not follow God's advice and marry a wife then your responsibility is to turn your spouse into a wife by adhering to God's holy advice and the power of His Holy Spirit to lead, guide and empower you to love your wife.

- Eph.5:26 to make her holy, cleansing her by the washing with water through the word.

Often our spouses are so far gone that your love, leadership, nor the Word of God will avail. The ship has so long ago sailed that we have lost all hope of ever turning our marriages around. We give up and turn everything over to God in prayer, and after you finish praying God turns it right back to you and tells you to clean her up.

> After you finish praying God turns it right back to you and tells you to clean her up.

Wife Defined: A wife is a woman who builds a nest for her family and cooperates with her husband. She understands that obedience and commitment is her duty and she must follow her husband as he follows Christ.

Spouse Defined: A spouse is a woman you have legally married who does not cooperate with you. She feels that your husbandry purpose is to make her happy; it's all about her!

Take note: In cleaning her up your job is not to make her happy because making her happy is not possible. Your job is to cleanse her with the washing of the Word of God. Forget the old mantra 'happy wife happy life'.

It has been reported that even NFL (G.O.A.T. quarterback) Tom Brady's wife supermodel Gisele Bündchen divorced him because he wanted to play his last year of football. One would have thought that being the G.O.A.T. would have cut him some slack but not for the modern feminist woman. She is myopic, only seeing the things she wants as opposite the things her husband and family need from her.

Her feminism will make her devalue then outright reject your masculinity. Gisele probably though she could find her true happiness in someone other than her husband to whom she had been married to for 13 years and had two children. It is commonly reported that she turned Tom in for a ju-jitsu instructor, feminists are transactional and they only care that the balance is weighed in their favor.

> The old mantra 'happy wife happy life' will surly lead you into a life of disrespect.

If you do everything to make her happy she will consider you to be a weak man which will cause her to disrespect you. The old mantra 'happy wife happy life' will surly lead you into a life of disrespect. Women desire a man all the while they attempt to turn you into something disgusting in their eyes, a wimp. And once they have achieved their goal of turning you into a wimp they will divorce you and begin their search for a strong man who will keep them under control for that type of man is who they actually want as a husband; a bronco buster not a tenderfoot. God created the woman for the man so it is her natural instinct to desire a man to pair-bond[46] with but the Genesis curse has doomed her to desire to control you. This bypolarism is the generator of many marital problems. She nags you or cuts you off sexually until you allow her to lead but when you do she becomes disgusted with you. In spite of her resistance to your leadership, in the long-run your best position is to always remain the leader.

<u>What are The Responsibilities of Marriage?</u>

When the Bible speaks of a wife's responsibility to her husband how does it define her responsibility? What is her role in the family? What does she bring to the table? What should you expect of her? What does the bible say you should expect of her. You should have been answering these questions long before you got married. If you knew the answers to these questions you probably would have made a better choice. Well it's all water under the bridge now, you got what you got, your work is cut out for you. But if you are free to marry another make sure she is a Tradwife:

There is a new term being bandied about in modern culture, it is Tradwife it means: a woman who believes in and practices traditional biblical and gender roles in marriages. Let's look at the 5 biblical roles of a godly wife/tradwife:

A Wife Is a Partner Who Rules With Her Husband

- Genesis 1:27-28, "So God created man in His own image; in the image of God He created him; male and female He created them. Then God blessed them, and God said to them, "Be fruitful and multiply; fill the Earth and subdue it; have dominion over the fish of the sea, over the birds of the air, and over every living thing that moves on the Earth."
- A wife neither rules over her husband nor is ruled by her husband, she rules alongside her husband. God created marriage to be a unity of cooperation where the goal is to raise a godly family that extends His kingdom.
    - Remember the Hebrew word rule means to have dominion over.

A Wife Is a Helper to Her Husband

- Genesis 2:18 The Lord God said, "It is not good for the man to be alone. I will make a helper suitable for him."
- The word 'helper' is not a term that implies 'submission' but is defined by the role God plays in the life of Israel. The word "helper" in Hebrew is "ezer", meaning a person who provides needed help and assistance. This word is used 21 times in the Old Testament, and 16 of those times refer to God. Its most memorable usage is found in Psalm 27:1 the Lord is my Helper.
- Your wife is no more subordinate to you than God is and her help should be valued as such.

A Wife Is the Crown of Her Husband

- Proverbs 12:4, "An excellent wife is the crown of her husband, but she who causes shame is like rottenness in his bones."
- What makes his wife his 'crown' is he trusts in her and she greatly enriches his life. She brings him good not harm all the days of her life. Because of what she does he is admired by all who know him and her children bless her and her husband praises her and she is greatly praised because of the type of wife she is.

A Wife Is To Submit To Her Husband

- Ephesians 5:22-24, "Wives, submit to your own husbands, as to the Lord. For the husband is head of the wife, as also Christ is head of the church; and He is the Savior of the body. Therefore, just as the church is subject to Christ, so let the wives be to their own husbands in everything".
- The word "submission" from the Greek "hypotasso" means to place or arrange under. God is very organized and as such He has an organization chart for the family where He places the husband as the leader. Now what is of particular interest is why God orders structure; it is because He holds the one He has been given the role of leader accountable to care for all those to whom he has been given the responsibility to lead.
- The husband is not greater or worth more than the wife then God the Father is not greater or more valuable than God the Son neither of which is greater or worth more than the Holy Spirit. When it comes to salvation their roles take structure and order. The Son, Jesus Christ takes orders from His Father and the Holy Spirit assists the Son as He leads the church.

A Wife Is a Builder of a Home (not house)

- Proverbs 14:1, "The wise woman builds her house, but the foolish pulls it down with her hands".
- In today's economy it is bandied about that each home needs two incomes to survive. This is not true. What each family needs is to lower their cravings for the creature comforts technology now affords us.
- Titus 2:4-8 These older women must train the younger women to love their husbands and their children, to live wisely and be pure, to work in their homes, to do good, and to be submissive to their husbands. Then they will not bring shame on the word of God. In the same way, encourage the young men to live wisely.
- A woman's place is in her home where she provides for her family care, warmth, nurture, peace, and organization. When she is forced out to her home to provide added income for unnecessary creature comforts then along with her wifely duties she typically puts in a 98 hour work week. That is not sustainable for anyone, no wonder she has issues with your leadership. Later we will take a look at what it actually takes to live in a one-income household. It is not impossible if your priorities are properly aligned with God's model of marriage.

> The Christian husband is to make his wife holy and clean, washed by the cleansing of God's word.

When the Bible speaks of a Husband's responsibility to his wife, how does it define that responsibility? The Christian husband is to make his wife holy and clean, washed by the cleansing of God's word and he does this with the attitude that places her benefit above his own. (Eph. 5:25-27). In other words, does the Bible teach that a husband should love his disobedient spouse? Of course he should because as her leader he is responsible to clean her up. He must love her but not necessarily the things that she does.

- Eph. 5:25 For husbands, this means love your wives, just as Christ loved the church. He gave up his life for her 'to make her holy and clean, washed by the cleansing of God's word. 27He did this to present her to himself as a glorious church without a spot or wrinkle or any other blemish.

By washing your spouse in the Word of God instead of her being this modern, feminist, western woman, she will be holy and without fault. Let it be said to all who have ears to hear; better to marry a wife than attempt to convert a spouse into one.

- Psalm 18:22 says: He who finds a wife finds what is good and receives favor from the LORD.

<u>It is Better to Marry a Wife than Attempt to Convert a Spouse</u>

The woman you marry should already be a wife. One of the first things I was taught in seminary by Dr. Howard Hendricks was this mantra 'As now so then' in his often quick and humorous style he was letting us know that our future was dictated by our present. In other words marry a wife not a spouse you feel has the potential to be a wife. A wife is not something a spouse learns from 'on the job training'. A wife is something from her youth she was raised to be. Now I'm not saying that if you have a wife you will not experience problems in your marriage but a wife will be committed to the marriage and your leadership of it.

Rather you have a spouse or a wife she suffers from the same curse. As part of the curse God placed upon Eve for her sin (Genesis 3:16), women by nature have a tendency to desire to rule over their husbands. And don't forget, that curse gave you a desire to rule over your wife.

- To rule: Is to require absolute submission without love as the guiding factor, this is satanic.
- To lead: God requires us to place her welfare before our own and act in love as our guiding factor. This is Christian

If you married wisely you picked a woman who has mastered abilities you are deficient in. It is the foolish husband who doesn't make use of those abilities. If you don't you will make the one she is supposed to be looking up to seem small and foolish all the while nurture rebellion. Wise leadership doesn't require that you make all the decision but that you are wise enough to give lead-way to your wife in areas she is better qualified in.

<u>Your Wife is not 'Other'</u>

You should never refer to your spouse as 'that woman' but as 'my woman'.

You should never refer to your spouse as 'that woman' but as 'my woman'. In the same way you would never refer to your broken arm as 'that arm' but 'my arm'. When God confronted Adam for disobeying Him, Adam's response was to blame his disobedience on that woman. He actually said 'the woman' but the implication was that she is not part of him. It was as if he had forgotten all about Gen. 2:24 where he said he and his wife were now 'one flesh'. I use the word 'that' to also convey the idea of 'other' in opposition to myself in the same manner as Adam conveyed the idea by saying 'with me'.

- Gen. 3:11b ...Have you eaten from the tree that I commanded you not to eat from?" 12The man said, "The woman you put here with me—she gave me some fruit from the tree, and I ate it."

Eve was wrong for enticing Adam to eat of the forbidden fruit but that she did it was not God's fault, it was Adam's fault because he stood by and did nothing. She was not 'that' woman but his woman because they were of one flesh. It was Adam who said in Gen. 2: 23

- The man said, "This is now bone of my bones and flesh of my flesh; she shall be called 'woman,' for she was taken out of man." 24That is why a man leaves his father and mother and is united to his wife, and they become one flesh.

An interesting concept 'one flesh', why doesn't God just pile some more dirt together and breath on it like He did to create Adam? Why does God make Eve come out of Adam instead? Why not make Eve separate from Adam? Why is she now bone of my bone and flesh of my flesh? Why are they now one flesh and not two separate fleshes? Why are you now bone of Adam's bone and flesh of Adam's flesh? When Adam sinned all that are associated with Adam took on his sin nature. Sinning doesn't make a person a sinner, it is because a person is a sinner that is why he/she sins. A person is a sinner because Adam's sin-nature passed onto all that came out of Adam, every human being came out of Adam, including Eve. Now Christ died for all the sins that resulted from being of the first Adam. Christ became the Last Adam that is just as the first Adam represented all of mankind so the Last Adam represents all of mankind. Christ becomes the Last Adam so He can pay the penalty for the sins of all who are associated with the First Adam. Christ could not die for the sins of the fallen angels because they have no representative head. Christ can die for the sins of mankind because we have a representative head, Adam. Just as the sin of one man passed unto the many so also by the righteousness of One Man salvation can pass unto all men. A man goes to Hell not because he is a sinner but because he has not accepted Jesus' payment for his sins. When Jesus is called the Last Adam that means He represents all that came through the First Adam, including Eve who of necessity if she were to receive salvation through Christ must also come through the First Adam. Hence God puts Adam to sleep and removes one of his (ribs) out of his body to make Eve so that Eve also like the rest of us came out of Adam.

- 1 Cor.15: 44b ...If there is a natural body, there is also a spiritual body. 45So it is written: "The first man Adam became a living being"; the last Adam, *(Jesus Christ)* a life-giving spirit. 46The spiritual did not come first, but the natural, and after that the spiritual. 47The first man was of the dust of the Earth; the second man is of heaven. 48As was the Earthly man, so are those who are of the Earth; and as is the heavenly man, so also are those who are of heaven. 49And just as we have borne the image of the Earthly man, so shall we bear the image of the heavenly man.

The image we bear of the Earthly man (Adam) is that of a sinner, unrighteous. The image we bear of the heavenly man (Jesus Christ) is that of a sinless person because Jesus pays the penalty for our sins and imputes to us His righteousness.

- 2 Cor. 5:21 God made him who had no sin to be sin for us, so that in him we might become the righteousness of God.

In order for God's righteousness to be imputed to Eve also she must come through Adam like us all.

- Rom. 5:17 For if, by the trespass of the one man, death reigned through that one man, how much more will those who receive God's abundant provision of grace and of the gift of righteousness reign in life through the one man, Jesus Christ! 18Consequently, just as one trespass resulted in condemnation for all people, so also one righteous act resulted in justification and life for all people. 19For just as through the disobedience of the one man the many were made sinners, so also through the obedience of the one man the many will be made righteous.

Well then since all men come through Adam and Christ represents all men that come through Adam then all men are saved? No! Yes, Jesus paid the penalty for all the sins of mankind but each and every man must chose to by faith accept the payment Jesus paid for you.

- Rom. 1:17 For in the gospel the righteousness of God is revealed—a righteousness that is by faith from first to last, just as it is written: "The righteous will live by faith.

Have you placed your trust in Jesus' payment for your sins, if so you can move onto the next session of this book? If not you and God need to have a talk about what you plan on doing with His Son, Jesus the Christ!

Now continuing God's thought in the fifth chapter of Ephesians:

- 28In the same way, husbands ought to love their wives as they love their own bodies. For a man who loves his wife actually shows love for himself. 29No one hates his own body but feeds and cares for it, just as Christ cares for the church. 30And we are members of his body. 31As the Scriptures say, "A man leaves his father and mother and is joined to his wife, and the two are united into one." 32This is a great mystery, but it is an illustration of the way Christ and the church are one. 33So again I say, each man must love his wife as he loves himself, and the wife must respect her husband.

Loving your wife by putting her first is only possible when you see your wife as your own body and as you would not cut of your own broken arm but mend it, in like manner you must also not divorce your broken spouse but rather mend her into being a wife.

> Divorce is not an option and that God expects your marriage to reflect His love.

God is saying that Eve would desire to rule over her husband, but her husband would instead rule over her. Is this what you are experiencing in your marriage? Is this the root of your marital problems? Are you both pig-headed and uncompromising? If so the future does not look prosperous for your marriage. But if you understand that divorce is not an option and that God expects your marriage to reflect His love for His Church then you must have the attitude that you and your wife are inseparable, that divorce is out of the question. So then pray while you lay hold of your burden and cleanse your spouse changing her from a modern feminist into a wife.

CHAPTER SIX

(The Matrix)

O.K. now after saying all that let's go back to 1 Peter 3:7 and delve into God's command to 'know' your wife. The fruit that a tree bears receives its nourishment through its root. The 'poisonous' fruit that a spouse bears gets its nourishment from the culture she was raised in. The 'nurturing' fruit that a wife bears gets its nourishment from the lessons she was taught from her godly parents as to how to be a wife. If the woman that you married was a wife then she would bear 'nurturing' fruit for you and her family, hands down but if she is bearing poisonous fruit then that is because she is not a wife but a spouse, hands down.

So then because you are reading this book it is safe to assume that you have married a spouse and the fruit she is bearing is poisonous. If you are to know your spouse you must know the culture she was planted in, where her roots draw its sustenance from. Again I refer back to 1 Peter because I want to remind you of what God first commands you to do to restore your marriage back to health.

- First Peter 3:7 You husbands in the same way, live with your wives in an understanding way, as with someone weaker, since she is a woman; and show her honor as a fellow heir of the grace of life, so that your prayers will not be hindered.

Ok, the scripture says to KNOW your wife/spouse. Though the NASB uses the word 'understand' the New Testament's original language uses the Greek word γνῶσις, its transliteration into English is gnosis, its definition is: knowledge. Some bible versions translate 1 Peter as 'dwell with your wives according to 'knowledge' (ASV). When we choose our spouses we didn't chose them 'according to knowledge' we chose them according a 'lust' that we confused as 'love'. The singing group 'The Platters' said it best back in the year 1958 with their hit song 'Smoke Gets In Your Eyes'

- They asked me how I knew my true love was true
- Oh-oh-oh-oh-oh, I, of course replied
- "Something here inside cannot be denied"
- They said, "Someday, you'll find all who love are blind
- So, I chaffed them, and I gaily laughed
- To think they could doubt my love
- Yet, today, my love has flown away
- Now, laughing friends deride tears I cannot hide
- Oh-oh-oh-oh-oh, so I smile and say
- "When a lovely flame dies
- Smoke gets in your eyes" (smoke gets in your eyes)
- Smoke gets in your eyes

> Neither husband nor wife should marry based on their perceived love or lust but out of commitment, duty, and honor.

When Jesus is about to say something monumental He prefaces His statement with the word 'truly' and sometimes He doubles up on the 'truly'. So here I use the word 'truly' and double it up 'truly, truly' neither husband nor wife should marry based on their perceived love or lust but out of commitment, duty, and honor. The infatuation of lust soon burns away and real love is something that increases over time and through hardship. But commitment, duty, and honor are a decision that is not based on circumstances, they will hold a marriage together even when a modern culture and society come against it.

Before 1965 marriages lasted 'until death did them part' back when they were arranged. But now that we date, commitment to marriage is almost non-existent. 'You asked me how I knew my true love was true, something deep inside cannot be denied'. You see the someday of the Platter's song has come 'Someday, you'll find all who love are blind' because when your heart is set on fire smoke gets in your eyes. You both were blinded by that smoke and when the blind lead the blind your marriage fell into the ditch.

My friend there was a time when your family would vet a potential mate for you because they knew with all your testosterone boiling over in your veins there was not enough blood left in your body to supply the cognitive functions of your brain. You both were blind so that neither of you two could see reality. Reality is what you missed all together and this chapter is designed to reveal to you the reality you should have been aware of.

<u>Welcome to Reality</u>

> You can't know your spouse until you know the culture her characteristics and proclivities were molded from.

In the Matrix movie Morpheus offers Neo a choice between taking the red pill or the blue pill. If he took the blue pill he could continue to live under the deception of the Matrix (a culture where modern feminism advances society) but because he chose the red pill, Neo became aware for the first time of the oppressive, parasitic culture of the Matrix (our contemporary feminist culture). When it comes to knowing your spouse God wants you to take the red pill. He says husbands KNOW your wives. You can't know your spouse until you know the culture her characteristics and proclivities were molded from, the root that nourished her bad disposition towards you and your marriage. Like on a Hollywood set you must look beyond the props to see what is real. The real world is revealed below[47]:

- Since 1965 an ever increasing number of women have been raised in dysfunctional homes. They have been raised in homes without the example of how a husband and his wife work together respecting each other and the lanes in which their respective roles function.

- They never learn how men think with logic and reason as opposed to how women think with their feelings. A truth you would be wise to consider in all of your discussions with your spouse.

- Modern women never learn who husbands are and as such diminish them to whom they want them to be; the person who is tasked with making them happy.

- With the absence of a father in these dysfunctional homes young girls do not have anyone to vet their potential mates and as such are left alone to their own immature desires. Confusing infatuation with love and not knowing that love is developed over time and comes from commitment to working through troubling times they give themselves to bad boys, pretty boys, and boys with pretty cars. These experiences lead to the emotional damage that results in the hatred, fear, and distrust of men you are experiencing.

- The modern woman not having been raised in a male led functional home along with a culture that promotes a feminism that has gone amuck, (they equate the duties of a wife with slavery) your spouse feels that the role of the wife is to be made happy by her husband. An impossible task that when not fulfilled by the husband the marriage is prone to divorce. The mantra "I can do bad all by myself" leads them to the divorce court where the laws of 'irreconcilable differences' favor them with child support and alimony of which the government takes their cut.

- The modern woman rejects the wife's traditional role of

keeping the family together during rough and disappointing times. They bad-mouth traditions not knowing that traditions are established for one simple reason; they work in keeping order in society.

- Feminism and materialism has driven mothers out of their homes and into the work place. This demise of traditional motherhood has had a deleterious effect on western culture.
    - Madonna said it best in her 1984 hit song "Material Girl". 'Cause we are living in a material world And I am a material girl.

- In the United States today, nearly 24 million children live in a single parent family. This total, which has been rising for half a century, covers about one in every three kids across America. A number of long term demographic trends have fueled this increase, including: marrying later, declining marriage rates, increasing divorce rates and an uptick in babies born to single mothers. Single parent families and especially mother only households are more likely to live in poverty compared to married parent households. Given this, kids of single parents are more likely to experience the consequences of growing up poor and being incarcerated. Children in poverty are more likely to have physical, mental and behavioral health problems, disrupted brain development, shorter educational trajectories, contact with the child welfare and justice systems, employment challenges in adulthood and more.[48]

- 41% of American mothers are single and unwed, the baby mama you married is accustomed to leading her family and when you come into the picture seeking to lead this new family she will resist relinquishing her headship. This coupled with her intrinsic fear of men and lack of trust in us will cause considerable problems.

When dealing with a woman like this let your yes be yes and your no be no. Let her get accustomed to you always doing what you say, and explain to her how your decision is best for her and the family.

- Women with children will always make her children her priority, get used to it. Women are nurturers, this is a good thing, though they should put the husband's concerns before their children their nurturing instincts will make them care for their children first, which as her leader who sacrifices himself for his family should be your desire.
- Children will react to you the way they see their mother reacting to you. So don't confront her with an issue you fear you may get push-back on in front of the children.

[Explain to your spouse the importance of your being a good father to her children depends on how she responds to you, especially in their presence.]

- As a by-product of the glorification of womanhood most women rate themselves as 10's (perfect) and therefore are delusional when they estimate their worth which causes confusion in their psyche resulting in:
  - Modern women feel their rightful place is to be pedestalized but when you pedestalize them they will think of you as less of a man.
  - When you treat them like queens even though they usurp your authority as king you will cause them to lose all respect for you.

- When they act like modern women but you treat them like they are traditional women they feel that you will accept all manner of disrespect.
- Modern women want the benefits of a traditional husband but do not want the responsibilities of a traditional wife.
  - Having rated themselves above their worth they surmise that you are not treating them good enough, or at the level of their misconceived worth.
  - Modern women desire a traditional man all the while they will attempt to turn you into a wimp, expecting of you to provide for their every desire even when they don't know what it is they want or need. They will be disappointed in you for not reading their minds and clairvoyantly doing the things that make them happy.
- Most western women will not see fault in themselves.
  - They feel, not rationalize, that if there is a problem in the marriage it will be your fault. They believe that "If you will just do what they want you to do everything will be perfect."
  - They believe the marriage is not working because you are not submitting to their instructions.
  - The song by Helen Reddy: 'I Am Woman' is the destructive delusion they bring to your marriage. Some stanzas are as follows: "I am woman hear me roar…, watch me grow, see me standing toe to toe…, but I'm still a little embryo with such a long, long way to go until I make my brother understand, Oh yes, I am wise but it's wisdom born of pain yes, I've paid the price but look how much I've gained if I

- have to, I can face anything I am strong (strong) I am invincible (invincible) I am woman.
  - The modern woman is under the delusion that they are strong and invincible, these characteristics are needed for a soldier at war but the characteristics needed for a wife is cooperative and submissive to God's marital order.
- Feminism and social media has warped their expectations.
  - Feminism wants equality only when it benefits the woman otherwise they feel it is best that a man keep his traditional role.
    - They want equal pay but the husband is responsible for all the bills.
    - They want you to answer that thump in the middle of the night.
    - She will want her own bank account but then will not leave yours alone. What's hers is hers but what's yours is hers also.
    - If war breaks out then it is just fine for her remain at home while the traditional man goes off to war and takes the bullet.
  - They want chivalry all the while they have killed chivalry
    - They treat nice guys as simps[49] or friend-zone them.
    - They want doors opened for them and always to be treated like a lady all the while emitting masculine vibes of domination.
  - The typical feminist spouse wants to take the lead until it all goes awry then they want you to step forward and implement the solution to the mess they have created.

- ◦ Feminism teaches the modern woman to be 'independent'. Their mantra is 'I don't need no man!' But the world operates from masculinity not femininity therefore when a woman feels she don't need man she must fulfill the necessary role of masculinity. In her mind this is preferable but if you have married her it is devastating. God has designed femininity and masculinity to complement each other and any other order is destructive to the marriage.
  - ◦ A lyric from Destiny's Child's hit record 'Independent Women' goes
    - ▪ Question, tell me what you think about me I buy my own diamonds and I buy my own rings Only ring your celly when I'm feelin' lonely When it's all over, please get up and leave.
  - ◦ But independence is anathema to the Christian model of marriage. Gen. 2:24 gives us a picture of the marriage bond before sin entered the world:

- • Gen. 2:24 That is why a man leaves his father and mother and is united to his wife, and they become one flesh.

"One flesh" echoes the language of the preceding verse when Adam first meets Eve and exclaims, "This one is bone of my bone, and flesh from my flesh!" (Genesis 2:23, NLT).

> Two becoming one in marriage involves uniting two whole and separate people into a new, God-designed and God-purposed life.

Two becoming one in marriage involves uniting two whole and separate people into a new, God-designed and God-purposed life. The two shall become one flesh clause expresses the original purpose of marriage: to seal a permanent relationship between a husband and wife.[50]

- Because the modern woman is independent she doesn't see her husband as a necessary part of her. He becomes dispensable and readily replaceable.
    - God created men and women to be together, modern feminism destroys that order resulting in the demise of the family unit.
    - It is after she divorces him that she finds out she has hit the wall[51] and when she can't readily replace him that she feels remorse and wants to come back to you. Unless you have remarried it is your Christian responsibility to take her back.

- 1 Cor. 7:10-11 Berean Literal Bible
    - 10Now to those having married I give this charge (not I, but the Lord): A wife is not to be separated from a husband. But if indeed she is separated, let her remain unmarried, or be reconciled to the husband; and a husband is not to send away a wife.

- Social media posts the perfect delusional life they want you to give them; full of international vacations, and perfect

obedient husbands.
  ○ Men who are six foot tall, six figure income, and six-
    pack abs
  ○ Private yacht vacations off the coast of Monte Carlo.

Modern women who have not experienced the married life in their youth are not aware that 'boredom' is an unescapable part of the married life. So when the inevitable boredom that creeps into every marriage takes place so does her disappointment which often is followed by divorce.

- It is common knowledge that the modern woman from their early teenage years until she hit the wall (35+) they desire three types of men because these men offer excitement:
  ○ 1. The bad boy
    ▪ After being rode hard by these guys they are the first to lose attraction.
  ○ 2. The cute guy
    ▪ After being cheated on so many times they are the second to lose attraction.
  ○ 3. The guy with access to money
    ▪ After being rejected so many times the desire for these guy's money have a power that is never diminished.
    ▪ Because men are no longer vetted for the modern woman she will suffer from the bad experiences of each.

- Dating these men will lead to disaster resulting in unwed motherhood, divorce, and emotional damage. The excitement these men offered will become imprinted on their psyche which will not allow them to tolerate boredom resulting in divorce. Unless she has had serious Christian therapy to erase these effects she will bring that damage into your marriage with her.

[As much as possible introduce your spouse to new experiences, this will raise your value to her. And keep her on the go to stave off boredom which will help in staving of divorce.]

Modern Feminism has maligned shame as a harmful emotion that has no place in a progressive society. But shame is an important emotion, when experienced in the right way is essential to a well-ordered society. Shame serves as brakes on antisocial and destructive behavior. With the removal of shame in our society we see the rise of out of wedlock pregnancies, ill-mannered youth, and ratchet behavior of women, crime and immoral behavior that is destroying all facets of society.

There was a time when a young girl got pregnant and because of the shame it brought to her family she was relocated to out of town relatives. Or the young couple was forced into marriage. These sever consequences inclined the young women to be more pure. But with the removal of shame unwed pregnancies have exploded and all the destruction on society that single mother homes result in is destroying our culture and your marriage.

The custom of shotgun marriage—vows taken, out of a sense of obligation, after an accidental pregnancy has occurred—plummeted as well: 43% of unwed pregnancies resulted in a shotgun marriage in the early 1960s; this is down to 9% today. Young couples today simply do not feel the need to marry when a baby enters the picture.

The percentage of all births to unmarried women declined slightly from 41% in 2009 to 40% in 2019. Between 2009 and 2019, the percentage of births to unmarried women among adolescents ages 15–17 increased from 94% in 2009 to 97% in 2019; among women ages 18–19, the percentage increased from 84% in 2009 to 88% in 2019.[52]

Since the free-love baby boomer generation modern women are promiscuous as such their high body count allows them to fantasize a composite lover with the best sexual attributes of those men they have slept with. You having married her now have to compete with that composite in her mind. Good luck!

Women with a higher body count also have higher divorce rates, cheat more often and experience an increased sensation of unhappiness.

Women with a higher body count also have higher divorce rates, cheat more often and experience an increased sensation of unhappiness.[53] With promiscuity comes the attraction for and imprinting of many sexual partners. Women with high body-counts are accustomed to changing partners whenever difficulties arise in a relationship. This is just one of the reasons why 70% - 90% of divorces are filed by women.

Research also indicates that imprinting helps to determine our sexual preferences as adults with regards to finding a partner, showing us the characteristics to search for in a potential mate. After orgasm, levels of vasopressin[54] rise in men; levels of oxytocin rise in women. These hormones are known to cause attachment and possession, and probably contribute to the feelings of closeness after sexual intercourse.

Females have higher levels of oxytocin than males, according to Markus MacGill, editor for Medical News Today, which is why they are more likely to feel an emotional connection with their partner. Having multiple sexual partners makes it difficult to sustain a healthy relationship because after many attachments the female brain becomes desensitized to oxytocin.

This is why when a woman is cheated on she asks her husband if he loves the woman he cheated with (she is concerned about his attachment to her) but if the man is cheated on he asks his wife if she had sex with him (he is concerned if she has given away what he is there to protect and defend). Though he should be more concerned about the effects of desensitization to oxytocin her brain experiences.

If you married a promiscuous woman you need to know that her brain is confused with the imprinting and attraction towards her previous multiple sex-partners.

The modern woman is addicted to attention that is why they spend so much time on the physical presentation. But if you give them too much attention your attention will lose value to them. When this happens they will treat you as if you don't matter and will seek it from someone else, someone new.

Women hate being rejected and often will adjust their attitude once you stop simping for them. Now I know this is confusing, women want your attention then they don't want your attention, they want you to give them all of your attention so they can reject your attention but if you stop giving them your attention they will do everything they can to regain your attention. This is why they are fascinated by the sigma male, he treats them as if his life will go on just fine without them.

Most woman raised under the western culture has issues that need professional CHRISTIAN therapy. Christian therapy because the word of God needs to be used in the cleansing process.

<u>Requiring Your Wife to Work is a Grave Mistake</u>

> If you can't afford to provide for her you can't afford to marry her.

If you can't afford to provide for her you can't afford to marry her. It is always better to marry a low-maintenance woman and keep her at that level than to marry a high-maintenance woman and attempt to lower her expectations.

Due to the Genesis curse the psychic of a spouse is to rule over her husband. Any lack in your husbandry will give her opportunity to emasculate you. To maintain a successful marriage with her you must exemplify the perfect godly husband. One of the attributes of the perfect godly husband, he is the provider.

Again, back in Genesis 3:16-20 where God passed judgment on their sin He punished the man with a different punishment than He did with the woman. To the woman He said she would suffer severely in childbirth and that she would seek to rule over her husband but to the man He said he would have to labor in painful toil all the days of his life. When we force our women to work we place a portion of our curse on her. Please note that after God passes out judgment on them Adam then names his wife. The naming of his wife shows that God's proclamation of Gen. 3:16b is fulfilled.

- ... Your desire will be for your husband, and he will rule over you."

Biblical names are given to establish authority over another. When you got married you changed her name, which showed your authority (leadership) over her and you gave her your name which identified her as a part of you, the bone of my bone and flesh of my flesh idea. This idea revealed that your authority over her was to be done in the sphere of love, care, and protection. In Genesis 2:15

- The LORD God took the man and put him in the Garden of Eden to work it and take care of it.

Adam was put over the Garden to care for it and to work it, that is to ʿābad, "to serve" it. In the same manner you are to care for and serve your wife.[55] Don't ask her to share in your burden but shield her from it.

Men of this modern generation when picking a wife often look for a partner, someone who can assist in the financial burden of a family. This is a grave mistake because you ask too much of her! You expect of her to be a traditional wife, turn your house into a home, raise your children, follow your leadership, and pay for the creature comforts you want to enjoy. Just how long do you think she will put up with that? Probably longer than she should. Just because you both entered into this misaligned agreement doesn't mean it is sustainable.

Because of the creature comforts of this modern age a two income family is required. It has not always been this way but we have come to think of two incomes as essential.

If you require your wife to work remember her definition of a husband is the one who provides to the marriage the three-legged stool of protection, provision, and leadership. In days of old protection was important because the state didn't provide it, now it does. Now a woman can walk at night from a club barely dressed and not fear assault. If you also remove provision from the equation by requiring her to work then their goes the second leg of the three legged stool. All you have left to your role as husband is leadership and that is directly proportional to how much you make more than her. What do I mean by this? One church business meeting early on my Christian path I heard a dear saintly woman stand up and shout to the deacons 'if you want to be big you have to pay big".

Hypergamy[56] has always and will always exist in a woman's psyche. Since she doesn't need you for protection; the removal of the first leg and she makes more than you; the removal of the second leg, provision then all she has left to ascribe your worth to the marriage is your leadership, and since she makes more than you she will not let you lead her; the removal to the third leg. There is nothing left that she needs from you. As a Christian Husband you don't want to be in the position where your wife feels that you bring nothing to the table.

As a side note the modern woman is annoyed when you ask them what they bring to the table but they definitely know what they want you to bring to the table.

She no longer depends on you for safety and you require her to work because you can't afford the creature comforts you both demand

and since you can't provide the creature comforts she desires she won't follow your leadership, what are you to do? First don't marry a woman you can't afford, marry one who is comfortable with less and then resist her demands for you to get her more stuff. Explain to her the reasons why you don't allow her to work and then hold your ground. Listen to Warren Buffet: "The key to a successful marriage is low expectations."

> The husband is the foundation of the family not the wife. It is his character and attributes that his family come to emulate through his leadership.

The husband is the foundation of the family not the wife. It is his character and attributes that his family come to emulate through his leadership. He must always be honest, moral, hard-working, faithful, trust-worthy and visionary. But how can he lead his wife if she has sold her allegiance to another man, her employer? He tells her he wants to see her at a certain time of the day for at least 40 hours a week and when she comes she must be presentable, obedient, pleasant, and work her butt off. He will accept no excuses for anything less than her high performance, maximum output, and total obedience to him. Then after 8 hours of work, two hours of travel and preparation you expect her to come home with a pleasant attitude, the woman is drained, disappointed, exhausted, and demoralized. Since marriages are transactional they must be balanced but for the woman who works she carries too much of the load.

In 1950 the average new home was 983 square feet and the average household 3.8 people. Today it's 2500 square feet and 2.6 people.

Modern housing are fancier: Central A/C, 2-3 car attached garages, swimming pools, high ceilings, granite countertops, finished basements, more bathrooms, massively decreased fire risk, higher capacity electrical circuits, improved water heaters, built-in appliances, etc.

Median home price in the US is $123/square foot. To house a family of four, <u>under 1950s standards</u> costs about $125,000 in America today. That's easily affordable to a single earner at the median full-time wage of $45,000/year.

Add to this multiple cars, computers and instead of one family television the average American home now has 2.93 TV sets per household.

If you want a godly wife and not a partner whose primary responsibility is to care for the home and not work outside of it both you and her need to be willing to sacrifice some creature comforts.

If you have chosen to operate a two-income home then be prepared to share in some of the household chores, knowing that your wife is the 'weaker vessel' be prepared to cut her some slack. When she gets home from work she is as tired as you are so as often as you can be willing to prepare a meal or wash the dishes or manage the kids while she relaxes in a bubble bath. Remember your broad shoulders are designed to bear the load not her narrow hips.

Be aware that feminism crept into our culture when women crept into the workplace and it will, if not already have, crept into your family unit when you required your wife to satisfy the demands of another man rather than the demands of your family unit.

<u>The Devastating Rise of Feminism</u>

It worked like this; Traditional Feminism demanded work place opportunity which removed from the three legged stool (protection, provision, and leadership) provision. Her entering the workplace led to her acquiring college degrees (90% of women who file for divorce have advanced degrees). Having divorced you she is now the head of a single mother home which led to the demise of the children[57].

- 63% of youth suicides are from fatherless homes (U.S. Dept. Of Health/Census) – 5 times the average.
- 90% of all homeless and runaway children are from fatherless

homes – 32 times the average.

- 85% of all children who show behavior disorders come from fatherless homes – 20 times the average. (Center for Disease Control)
- 80% of rapists with anger problems come from fatherless homes –14 times the average. (Justice & Behavior, Vol. 14, p. 403-26)
- 71% of all high school dropouts come from fatherless homes – 9 times the average. (National Principals Association Report)[58]

So then Traditional Feminism led to the destruction of the Christian home and demise of the children. Traditional Feminism morphed into Modern Feminism which has destroyed the very culture of the nation.

A major target of Modern Feminism is the reduction of shame. Women are encouraged to live their 'best lives' and not allow shame to restrict their sexual fantasies. Shame is a product of a society that prioritizes the soul over the body and is a defense mechanism against all that is low, vulgar, and sinful. Since women are the custodians of the culture the loss of shame promoted by modern feminism in today's world comes from a profound change in women's moral values.

Feminism takes marriage and replaces it with solitude. It takes children and replaces them with empty wombs and hearts. It takes education and turns it into a life of enslavement, and it takes careers and turns them into the purpose of life. This ideology is a poison. No society can live long when drinking it. Ladies and gentlemen, the problem in America is not masculinity, nor is it the nuclear family, nor is it the prospect of traditional gender roles. No, the toxic thing here, is feminism.[59]

<u>Don't Marry an Idle Woman</u>

A traditional wife is a rare treasure because in her God finds His fulfillment for the family and moral conduct for a society that promotes His Kingdom. Anything that destroys the family is anathema to God. Feminism destroys the family.

But also know that if you seek the traditional wife who has your children and stays home make sure she is a Christian wife committed to her family unit for if she redefines her 'best life' as being without you the alimony and child support you pay her will be prohibitive.

A wife working outside of her home is a recent social development, this primarily because a wife's home duties were more than enough to keep her busy. Just putting a meal on the table was a major effort. Working the family garden, wringing the neck of a chicken, plucking its feathers, milking the cows, starting a fire and standing over it until the chicken was baked was no small task. Think of cleaning the cloths, no indoor plumbing, no washing machine, no electric iron, hanging the wash on an outdoor line and hoping it doesn't rain. Making soap, no refrigerator, no quick run to the county store because it was too far away. Seven or eight children to look after, make sure they did their chores, on and on and on but now a woman whose job is the care of her home will have time on her hands. Beware, idle hands are the devil's workshop.

- 1 Tim. 5:13 Besides, they get into the habit of being idle and going about from house to house. And not only do they become idlers, but also busybodies who talk nonsense, saying things they ought not to.

Today idleness looks like: avoiding spiritual self-improvement, lazy, no purpose in what is done, pointlessly spending time doing nothing, allowing their days to be filled with social media scrolling, gossip, shopping, middle of the day gathering with other lazy women, entertainment television, and other worldly useless pleasures.

A wise husband encourages his wife to spend her idle time in the Lord's work. His wife devotes her idle time to serving the Lord in ministries that care for the indigent, teach children God's commands, and support the different offices of the Church.

Marriages are too easy to enter, there was a better time when one's family had the responsibility to vett the betrothed and if they were not satisfied the marriage was off. Family members are not infatuated by beauty as men are and so it is best that the cooler heads of families prevail. The times are long gone when a man brought his girlfriend home and the women took her aside and gave her the once over. And if she didn't meet their approval they ran her off. But since feminism has enter the culture it has destroyed the family, the one check on faulty marriages.

Are you sorry you picked the 'red pill', is its reality too stark for your taste? Has it left you feeling hopeless and helpless? Are you now realizing that you should not have married the spouse you chose? Have you watched the movie 'Matrix' if so is your reality as bleak as in the movie? Do you wish you had taken the 'blue pill', well you can't un-see what the 'red-pill' has revealed to you? Stark isn't it? All is not lost, God is still on His throne.

CHAPTER SEVEN

(This is too much I give up)

I know, we as godly husbands cry along with Louis Armstrong as he sung his hit song - Nobody Knows the Trouble I've Seen (1962), but this is not true. Sure the actions of your modern, western, feminist spouse has been so displeasing that your anger burns against her. She is not what was advertised to you and now you want out of the deal. God knows the feeling for He also was displeased with His spouse Israel.

- Isaiah 54:5 For your Maker is your husband, the LORD of hosts is his name; and the Holy One of Israel is your Redeemer, the God of the whole Earth he is called.

God caught His wife Israel in the act of adultery which is equated with her act of idolatry. When you turn from God by ascribing His blessings to you by other means then that is an act of spiritual adultery.

- Ex. 32:7 Then the Lord said to Moses, "Go down, because your people, whom you brought up out of Egypt, have become corrupt. 8They have been quick to turn away from what I commanded them and have made themselves an idol cast in the shape of a calf. They have bowed down to it and sacrificed to it and have said, 'These are your gods, Israel, who brought you up out of Egypt.'

And like you, in Exodus 32 starting in verse 9, all God wanted to do was to get rid of her:

- "I have seen these people," the Lord said to Moses, "and they are a stiff-necked people. 10Now leave me alone so that my anger may burn against them and that I may destroy them.

Then I will make you into a great nation." 11But Moses sought the favor of the Lord his God. "Lord," he said, "why should your anger burn against your people, whom you brought out of Egypt with great power and a mighty hand? 12Why should the Egyptians say, 'It was with evil intent that he brought them out, to kill them in the mountains and to wipe them off the face of the Earth'? Turn from your fierce anger; relent and do not bring disaster on your people. 13Remember your servants Abraham, Isaac and Israel, to whom you swore by your own self: 'I will make your descendants as numerous as the stars in the sky and I will give your descendants all this land I promised them, and it will be their inheritance forever.' " 14Then the Lord relented and did not bring on his people the disaster he had threatened.

In the midst of God's anger Moses petitioned God to be merciful because it was God who chose Israel to be His wife (vs.11) in the same manner that you chose your spouse. Also God's reputation would be ruined (vs.12) in the eyes of the world because the husband who divorces his wife deals treacherously towards her, the same as your reputation will be towards the spouse you divorce.[60] Then Moses reminded God of the promises He made concerning her (vs. 14). You too should remember the promises you made to her and God.[61] After Moses plea for mercy God took another course of action[62] and as always He chose to be merciful even in the midst of His anger. You also are to be merciful even in the midst of your anger.

- Rom. 12:17 Do not repay anyone evil for evil. Be careful to do what is right in the eyes of everyone.

> He does not command you to do what you can't but He does require you to walk the path He has prepared and enabled you to.

I know you're saying "I'm not God" but you are called to imitate Him. He does not command you to do what you can't but He does require you to walk the path He has prepared and enabled you to. You say you still don't have ears to hear, well let's look at it another way. You're thinking "since the modern woman I married is so detestable why not just divorce my spouse and get myself a wife?"

<u>It is Cheaper to Keep Her</u>

Make no mistake in every state 'divorce laws' favor the woman, even if she is found to be in the wrong, even if she cheated on you and blamed you for not fulfilling her emotional needs and then filed for divorce. Even if you exercised your God given option for divorce, alimony and child support still can be more formidable than when Johnny Taylor's song 'cheaper to keep her' was released 50 years ago.

The reason many women do not want you to write a prenuptial contract is because they already have a better one written for them by the State. Also if you were wise enough to have your marriage to this modern feminist woman contingent on her signing a prenuptial contract be aware that they are routinely broken. And if the wife seeks to break the prenuptial often the husband must pay for her attorney fees.

Rapper Jeezy filed for divorce from TV personality Jeannie Mai Jenkins after two years of marriage. Though he and his spouse Mai signed a prenuptial she contested that prenuptial she agreed with for over three years at Jeezy's expense, he had to pay nearly one million dollars in legal fees.

Before you sign a marriage contract it probably is wise to consult with a 'divorce attorney' so that you might gain some understanding of the obligation you are signing up for. Obligations like any asset you or your spouse acquire or earn during the marriage become marital property or commingling of marriage assets (you pay any portion of the mortgage on the family home your parents left you and your siblings with the earnings from your employment) becomes her property also.

The better way to prepare a prenuptial is to do it collaboratively. Do it where you both have an opportunity to talk about what your expectations are concerning your new status as 'husband and wife' and how you will handle property issues upon death or divorce.

> Consulting a divorce attorney before you get married will open the door for you two to have important conversations about awkward topics you avoided.

Meeting with a divorce lawyer before you get married will help both of you understand how your relationship, money, and lives will change after you say 'I Do'. Best of all consulting a divorce attorney before you get married will open the door for you two to have important conversations about awkward topics you avoided or didn't know you needed to have. Most importantly a discussion with a divorce attorney may reveal many hidden motivation for matrimony. Of course you both intend for the marriage to last forever but it is a fool who doesn't take into account half the couples who got married intended their marriages to last forever. Just saying if 50% of airplanes fall out of the sky it is best to pack a parachute.

<u>The Woman God Married Was a Mess Too</u>

To give up on your marriage is to make the same mistake you made when you married her, not following God's advice. God hates divorce and so to give up on your spouse is to give up on God's ability to perform a miracle in your marriage.

Have you ever heard of the woman God married? Her name was Gomer, and her story is told in the Book of Hosea, please read the whole book to see what God put up with in His own decrepit marriage so that in the end He would have a faithful wife.

Gomer in the Bible was the unfaithful wife of Hosea the prophet. The Lord used Hosea and Gomer's relationship as an object lesson to show how Israel had sinned against Him by following other gods and how God remains faithful even when His people don't. God uses this relationship as an object lesson for you who have unfaithful and idle spouses, a lesson for us not to give up on them. God will never give up on us, just as Hosea didn't give up on Gomer. God continues to love his people even when they sin, in like manner we are never to give up on our marriages.

God gave Hosea an unusual command:

- When the LORD first began speaking to Israel through Hosea, he said to him, "Go and marry a prostitute, so that some of her children will be conceived in prostitution. This will illustrate how Israel has acted like a prostitute by turning against the LORD and worshiping other gods." (NLT Hosea 1:2).

After bearing three children, Gomer left Hosea to return to her former life of prostitution.

God then gave Hosea another, even more amazing, command:

- "Go, show your love to your wife again, though she is loved by another man and is an adulteress. Love her as the Lord loves the Israelites, though they turn to other gods" (Hosea 3:1).

Hosea obeyed, buying his wife back with fifteen shekels of silver and some barley (verse 2). This is the type of love that God requires of us to have for our spouses. Our love is to be undeterred by her unfaithfulness.[63] The love we are to have for our spouses is to reflect God's love for His wayward, idolatrous people.

Hosea says that God will remove the names of the Baals from Israel's mouth and betroth her to Him forever, in righteousness and justice, in steadfast love and mercy (Hosea 2:17, 19). God will heal them by His own power (Hosea 14:4–7). We too are also to remove the evil in our spouses by God's power assessed by prayer, and obedience to His Words of Wisdom.

Though your friends and family encourage you to give up on your wayward wife don't give up on God. As God told Jairus in Luke 8:49

- While Jesus was still speaking, someone came from the house of Jairus, the synagogue leader. "Your daughter is dead," he said. "Don't bother the teacher anymore." 50 Hearing this, Jesus said to Jairus, "Don't be afraid; just believe, and she will be healed."

Jairus' had gone to Jesus with the request that Jesus save his daughter from dying. While on their way to his daughter it was reported to Jairus, he need not bother Jesus anymore because his daughter had died. 50Hearing this, Jesus said to Jairus, "Don't be afraid; just believe, and she will be healed."

Like Jairus Jesus speaks the same words to us 'Don't be afraid; just believe, and she will be saved. Though like Jairus' daughter your marriage may be dead if you bring Jesus to the problem He can breathe life back into it like He brought life back into Jairus' daughter.

> However much God hates the wickedness of your spouse He hates divorce more.

Just how much are we to put up with, you may ask? However much God hates the wickedness of your spouse He hates divorce more. Do not become weary of the foolishness you are called to endure but take heart in being obedient to God.

- Galatians 6:9 Let us not become weary in doing good, for at the proper time we will reap a harvest if we do not give up.

- 1 Cor. 7:10 (BLB) Now to those having married I give this charge (not I, but the Lord): A wife is not to be separated from a husband. 11But if indeed she is separated, let her remain unmarried, or be reconciled to the husband; and a husband is not to send away a wife.
- Malachi 2:16 (NASB) "For I hate divorce," says the LORD, the God of Israel, "and him who covers his garment with wrong," says the LORD of hosts. "So take heed to your spirit, that you do not deal treacherously."
  - 'Garment' is a metaphor for spouse
  - "Hate" (from śānēʾ) means to detest
  - Treacherously: The act of hating by divorcing your wife because the one you are to protect you act violently towards by divorcing her.

God hates divorce because the man who divorces his wife deals treacherously with her. Everyone likes to believe in their own eyes that they have suffered more than anyone else in marriage and therefore are justified in their divorce. And even if this is so still it doesn't matter because God judges not from your eyes but His own and in His eyes if you divorce your wife you are doing evil.

I know that this is a hard saying to hear but as God has often said "he who has ears to hear let them hear".

This may help you to hear; you picked her she is yours, you didn't follow God's advice when you picked her don't make the same mistake now by rejecting God's advice and divorce her.

Okay, I didn't marry well so am I truly stuck with this miserable woman? Whatever grounds the Bible possibly gives for divorce, does not mean God desires a divorce to occur. There are two grounds for divorce God allows:

- (1) sexual immorality Matthew 5:32 and 19:9
    - 5:32 But I tell you that anyone who divorces his wife, except for sexual immorality, makes her the victim of adultery, and anyone who marries a divorced woman commits adultery.
    - 19:9 I tell you that anyone who divorces his wife, except for sexual immorality, and marries another woman commits adultery."
- (2) abandonment by an unbeliever 1 Corinthians 7:15-16

- But if the unbeliever leaves, let it be so. The brother or the sister is not bound in such circumstances; God has called us to live in peace. 16How do you know, wife, whether you will save your husband? Or, how do you know, husband, whether you will save your wife?

God May Allow Divorce but Not Sanction Re-marriage

> God always wants to keep open the option of mending the marriage, even after a divorce occurs.

Acknowledgment, forgiveness, reconciliation, and restoration are always the first steps. Divorce should only be viewed as a last resort and then only in case of the two above exclusions. Now understand, just because God allows divorce doesn't mean that He sanctions re-marriage. God always wants to keep open the option of mending the marriage, even after a divorce occurs.

- Luke 16:18. "Whoever divorces his wife and marries another commits adultery; and whoever marries her who is divorced from her husband commits adultery."

There is only one situation in which God sanctions re-marriage to another woman.

- Duet. 24:1-4a If a man marries a woman who becomes displeasing to him because he finds something indecent about her, and he writes her a certificate of divorce, gives it to her and sends her from his house, 2and if after she leaves his house she becomes the wife of another man, 3and her second husband dislikes her and writes her a certificate of divorce, gives it to her and sends her from his house, or if he dies, 4then her first husband, who divorced her, is not allowed to marry her again after she has been defiled. That would be detestable in the eyes of the Lord.

Here we see the only case where God does not desire the re-establishment of a broken marriage, in every other case He desires the re-establishment of the broken marriage.

Being single should not be viewed as a curse or punishment, but as an opportunity to serve God wholeheartedly (1 Corinthians 7:32-36). God's command in 1 Cor. 7:9 that 'it is better to marry than to burn with passion' is spoken to the unmarried not the divorced for Luke 16:18. "Whoever divorces his wife and marries another commits adultery; and whoever marries her who is divorced from her husband commits adultery."

If you are divorced or never married God's ideal for you would be with His help, to control your sexual passions and then give your life to serving God.

The reason God created mankind was so that mankind could experience God's Love, this is God's goal for your life. Since everything that God commands you to do originates out of His love for you the only way your life can fully experience God's love is that your life is lived fully obedient to His commands. Any disobedience to God's commands moves the center of our experience of God from His love to His mercy. This is why the more we sin (disobey God) the further we feel apart from Him.

You didn't start your courtship out in the direction you wanted to go. You wooed her, told her she was perfect for you, and you gave her whatever she wanted and now you are reaping what you sowed and want to turn your marriage around. I don't blame you for wanting to turn your marriage around but you helped create this monster and with God's help you can turn your monstrous marriage around. But in the same manner that you can't turn an aircraft carrier around on a dime, you can't turn your marriage around on a dime neither, it takes a lot of prayer, understanding, and preparation.

If you want to turn your marriage around God requires of you to:

- 1 Peter 3:7 says, "HUSBANDS, LIVE WITH YOUR WIVES IN AN UNDERSTANDING WAY, showing honor to the woman as the weaker vessel, since they are heirs with you of the grace of life, so that your prayers may not be hindered"

What does it mean to "SHOW HONOR TO THE WOMAN AS THE WEAKER VESSEL" It means your responsible is to:

- Eph. 5:25-28 Husbands, love your wives, just as Christ loved the church and gave himself up for her 26to make her holy, cleansing her by the washing with water through the word, 27and to present her to himself as a radiant church, without stain or wrinkle or any other blemish, but holy and blameless. 28In this same way, husbands ought to love their wives as their own bodies. He who loves his wife loves himself.

Dr. Tony Evans testimony is that when his father became saved the Christian life his father lived turned his mother around from being argumentative to desiring the peace she saw in her husband. His Christian father could do what his natural father could not, that is bring peace and order to his family through the guidance of the Holy Spirit. He became a changed man and that changed his whole family.

Be God's man to receive God's blessings. Dr. Tony Evans father became God's man in the midst of a troubled marriage and God blessed not only his wife but his family and not only his family but the whole world through Dr. Tony Evans world-wide ministries. There is so much more on the line than just your feelings, God is desirous to do a work through you and your family, you just have to have eyes to see and ears to hear.

- 1 Cor. 2:9 However, as it is written: "What no eye has seen, what no ear has heard, and what no human mind has conceived" — the things God has prepared for those who love him—

If you have married a modern, western, feminist woman then you have a battle on your hands but not on your hands alone for Jesus is there to share the burden with you. Don't buckle under the load many have carried greater. The poetry of Annie Johnson Flint can lighten any night of despair. Her own parents had died in her childhood, and her foster parents both passed away also. Her one sister was very frail and struggling to meet her own situation bravely. Annie suffered from a debilitating arthritis which would not allow her to work. But in the midst of her struggles she wrote many poems but the one that should encourage you not to give up is: 'He Giveth More Grace'

1. He giveth more grace as our burdens grow greater, He sendeth more strength as our labors increase; To added afflictions He addeth His mercy, To multiplied trials He multiplies peace.

2. When we have exhausted our store of endurance, When our strength has failed ere the day is half done, When we reach the end of our hoarded resources Our Father's full giving is only begun.

3. Fear not that thy need shall exceed His provision, Our God ever yearns His resources to share; Lean hard on the arm everlasting, availing; The Father both thee and thy load will upbear.

4. His love has no limits, His grace has no measure, His power no boundary known unto men; For out of His infinite riches in Jesus He giveth, and giveth, and giveth again.

CHAPTER EIGHT

(Remarriage is not an option)

<u>Looking for the Virtuous Wife</u>

If you are reading this book in anticipation of getting married to a wife, pray to God for His favor.

- Psalm 18:22 He who finds a wife finds what is good and receives favor from the Lord.

Though most people assume the right to divorce includes the right to remarry most of the verses on divorce in the bible don't speak to the issue of remarriage but Deuteronomy 24:1-4 does. The passage tells us that a man or woman cannot return to a former spouse and re-marry him or her if the former spouse had subsequently married another person. But if your previous spouse has not remarried and she desires to reconcile with you then you must be reconciled back to her.

- Deut. 24:1 If a man marries a woman who becomes displeasing to him because he finds something indecent about her, and he writes her a certificate of divorce, gives it to her and sends her from his house, 2and if after she leaves his house she becomes the wife of another man, 3and her second husband dislikes her and writes her a certificate of divorce, gives it to her and sends her from his house, or if he dies, then her first husband, who divorced her, is not allowed to marry her again after she has been defiled. That would be detestable in the eyes of the Lord.
- 1 Cor. 7:10 (BLB) Now to those having married I give this charge (not I, but the Lord): A wife is not to be separated from a husband. 11But if indeed she is separated, let her remain unmarried, or be reconciled to the husband; and a

husband is not to send away a wife.

But if your previous spouse has remarried then you are free from her to marry another woman. If you should choose to do so don't make the same mistake as before and not follow God's advice. His advice is like guard-rails to keep you on the one and true marriage track. Any crossing outside of His guard-rails will lead to the same result as before.

> God will not pick your wife, He didn't pick the last one you had and He is not taking responsibility for picking the next one you fall in heat with.

God will not pick your wife, He didn't pick the last one you had and He is not taking responsibility for picking the next one you fall in heat with. But He has given you His marriage guard-rails to keep you on track towards a godly woman. The very first thing we do when picking a wife is to go outside of God's guide-rail, we look on the outside instead of on the inside of the woman.

First and foremost don't get caught up in her physical beauty but seek one with noble character. A good wife is a treasure and if she is a virtuous type woman then she is the rarest of treasures.

Jacob got caught-up in Rachel's beauty:

- Gen. 29:16 Now Laban had two daughters. The older daughter was named Leah, and the younger one was Rachel. 17There was no sparkle in Leah's eyes, but Rachel had a beautiful figure and a lovely face. (NLT).

Rachel caused Jacob many problems over their marriage but Leah was of a noble character and birthed him many sons. God reveals His honor for one and displeasure on the other by how He buries them.

Rachel died giving birth to her second child, Benjamin and was buried on the way to Bethlehem but Leah was buried in the same tomb as Abraham and Sarah and Isaac and Rebekah also Jacob and his son Joseph would later be buried in this tomb as well.

I know men look on the outside and if the woman is not pleasing to the eyes then she is overlooked for marriage. But we will be wise to understand how God selects:

- 1 Samuel 16:7 But the LORD said to Samuel, "Do not consider his appearance or his height, for I have rejected him. The LORD does not look at the things people look at. People look at the outward appearance, but the LORD looks at the heart."

As men we want someone who is beautiful, fit, friendly, cooperative, submissive, and wise in the ways of God. These first two requirements are outside appearance[64] the latter four are internal. Over time a man will come to love a woman who is friendly, cooperative, submissive and wise in the ways of God but if she is only fit and beautiful then his infatuation will never turn into love. We like God should focus on the heart. Her beauty is attractive but it comes with certain baggage; the constant approach of men everywhere she goes, an over valuation of her worth, an expectation of the 'pretty privilege'[65] she has experienced all her life. In a marriage these things will cause a 10 to be reduced to a 0 because as a wife though beautiful she will never allow peace to matriculate in your marriage.

> Samson is the perfect picture
> of a man whom God had
> great plans for being reduced
> by the subduction of a
> beautiful woman.

Don't be like Samson, in the bible the first words of Samson are "I have seen a Philistine woman in Timnah; now get her for me as my wife." (Judges 14:2b) His wife Delilah is the perfect picture of a 10 turning into 0. Samson is the perfect picture of a man whom God had great plans for being reduced by the seduction of a beautiful woman.

Take note of God's word and don't be fooled like young men are. Solomon the wise warns the young men of the immoral woman in the book of Proverbs (ch.2; 5;7). This woman represents primarily the prostitute and the illegitimate wife (ch.7:10). She is characterized by using smooth words to appeal to the weakness of mankind (ch.2:16; 5:3; 7:21). Cunningly, she claims to be moral (ch.7:14) and assures her victim of his safety (verse 19, 20).[66]

Solomon uses an illustration to emphasize his instruction (ch.7). He speaks of the immoral woman who had roamed the streets looking for a victim and once she finds him, "She persuades him with the greatness of her teachings; with her smooth lips she compels him. He goes after her suddenly; like an ox to the slaughter he goes, and like a stag to the instruction of a fool, until an arrow pierces his entrails, like a bird rushing into a snare, but he does not know that it will cost him his life" (Proverbs 7:21-23).

As for the young man in Solomon's illustration[67], he is typical of many moral offenders today, who, while permitting unwise associations, having no intention at first of selling their soul to lust. But suddenly they find themselves in a trap from which they seem powerless to escape. These foolish young men should have successfully repulsed the first instigation of evil. The Bible teaches, "Touch not;

taste not; handle not" (Colossians 2:21) is the only safe course to pursue in such situations.

Just as the virtuous woman is the personification of God's wisdom the immoral woman is the personification of the foolishness of man's wisdom. It is like a metaphor or a parable in that it relies on what is known to reveal what is not apparent. The man who marries the wisdom of the world is like a man who marries an immoral wife she will bring destruction upon his own life and home. In like manner the man who marries God's wisdom is like the man who marries a virtuous wife, she will bring him good all the days of her life.

The immoral woman is certainly not one of the "keepers at home" that Paul commended in Titus 2:3-5:

- 3 Older women likewise are to be reverent in their behavior, not malicious gossips nor enslaved to much wine, teaching what is good, 4so that they may encourage the young women to love their husbands, to love their children, 5to be sensible, pure, workers at home, kind, being subject to their own husbands, so that the word of God will not be dishonored.

Paul advised that a godly man will keep himself from temptation and trials of such a woman in 1 Corinthians 6:18-20:

- 18 Flee sexual immorality. Every other sin that a person commits is outside the body, but the sexually immoral person sins against his own body. 19Or do you not know that your body is a temple of the Holy Spirit within you, whom you have from God, and that you are not your own? 20For you have been bought for a price: therefore glorify God in your body.

> Then after the foolish male mates with her she turns around and devours him.

The modern woman dresses promiscuously and shares her wares freely like the female black widow spider who during peak mating season as thousands of males prowl around looking for females she spins out her silk pheromone-laced web to attract males. Then after the foolish male mates with her she turns around and devours him. Many a foolish man has married such a woman who first emasculates his spirit then devours him in divorce court.

But you my friend should run from her as Joseph did from Potiphar's wife (Genesis 39:12). And the scent of her perfume should remind you of the female black widow spider's pheromone. "Therefore let him who thinks he stands take heed lest he fall" (1 Corinthians 10:12). The wise man knows that he can't build a home and family with these foolish feminist women because they will:

- Proverbs 14:1 'The wise woman builds her house, but with her own hands the foolish one tears hers down.

The wise woman listens to the word of God but the foolish woman listens to her feminist friends who have torn down their own homes, not understanding that who you befriend you become.

- I Cor. 15:33 Do not be misled: "Bad company corrupts good character." 34Come back to your senses as you ought, and stop sinning; for there are some who are ignorant of God—I say this to your shame.

Since modern feminists never experience a good, functional relationship with a father, brother or uncle they don't value relationships where men lead. They will always have a negative opinion of the direction you are leading the relationship.

- Test your lady-friend to see if she quietly follows your leadership or has a lot of push-back.
    - 1 Peter 3:3-4 Your beauty should not come from outward adornment, such as elaborate hairstyles and the wearing of gold jewelry or fine clothes. 4Rather, it should be that of your inner self, the <u>unfading beauty of a gentle and quiet spirit</u>, which is of great worth in God's sight.
- A mouthy lady-friend will become a nagging spouse.
    - Proverbs 21:9 — 'Better to live on a corner of the roof than share a house with a quarrelsome wife.'
    - Proverbs 21:19 — 'Better to live in a desert than with a quarrelsome and nagging wife.

<u>God's Wisdom has a Beauty All its Own</u>
The wise woman is a treasure and like all treasures they are rare and hard to find. Be diligent in your search, be not fooled by the shininess of fool's gold as many of us were.

God says what is of great worth: beauty that comes from one's inner self, an unfading beauty that comes from a gentle and quiet spirit.

- 1 Peter 3:3 Your beauty should not come from outward adornment, such as elaborate hairstyles and the wearing of gold jewelry or fine clothes. 4Rather, it should be that of your inner self, the unfading beauty of a gentle and quiet spirit, which is of great worth in God's sight.

Notice that this 'inner-beauty' is 'unfading'. It is of 'great worth' because it is like wine that gets better and better as it ages. It is unlike physical-beauty that ages like 'milk'.

In church today I saw an old man who obviously was suffering from a stroke struggle to take the seat just in front of me. One minute later his wife came and snuggled up to him sharing their warmth, it is often cold in my church. It was a touching and heartwarming scene. It made me wonder how many modern feminist women would have just divorced him in his time of need. This is the culture we live in, traditional women are few and far in-between and we are called to suffer with what is insufferable. Before you consent to marrying a woman of these later generations test to see if she carries a temperament of vindictiveness, tell her 'NO' and examine her response. If she suggests a different direction while being submissive to you then great she has her own mind and will be useful to the marriage because she will be able to show you another view point. But if she insists on you following her lead then she is just a spouse and will resist your every attempt to lead your family.

If you have a traditional Christian wife cherish her as a jewel of great price. As men to our own detriment we are drawn to what pleases our eyes but the virtuous type woman brings so much more to the table than what is fleeting (physical beauty).

Proverbs 31:10...31:

- 10An excellent wife, who can find her? For her worth is far above jewels. 11The heart of her husband trusts in her, and he will have no lack of gain. 12She does him good and not evil all the days of her life. 13She looks for wool and linen, And works with her hands in delight. 14She is like merchant ships; she brings her food from afar. 15And she rises while it is still night and gives food to her household, And portions to her attendants. 16She considers a field and buys it; from her earnings she plants a vineyard. 17She surrounds her waist with strength and makes her arms strong. 18She senses that her profit is good; her lamp does not go out at night. 19She stretches out her hands to the distaff, and her hands grasp the spindle. 20She extends her hand to the poor, and she stretches out her hands to the needy. 21She is not afraid of the snow for her household, for all her household are clothed with scarlet. 22She makes coverings for herself; her clothing is fine linen and purple. 23Her husband is known in the gates, when he sits among the elders of the land. 24She makes linen garments and sells them, and supplies belts to the tradesmen. 25Strength and dignity are her clothing, and she smiles at the future. 26She opens her mouth in wisdom, and the teaching of kindness is on her tongue. 27She watches over the activities of her household, And does not eat the bread of idleness. 28Her children rise up and bless her; Her husband also, and he praises her, saying: 29"Many daughters have done nobly, But you excel them all." 30Charm is deceitful and beauty is vain, But a woman who fears the LORD, she shall be praised. 31Give her the product of her hands, and let her works praise her in the gates.

> Charm and Beauty are not the ideal for marriage but a good wife is indispensable.

Charm and Beauty are not the ideal for marriage but a good wife is indispensable. A fulfilling and successful marriage is one where husbands and wives submit to one another.

Eph. 5:21 Submit to one another out of reverence for Christ.

How to Know She is Wife Material

Now to the men who are seeking marriage how do you know if the woman who has captured your eye is a wife or something more cherished a virtuous woman?

Whomever she may be make sure the woman you want wants you. Make sure she is in love with your character, personality, ethos or as the bible describes it your 'heart' and not just your provisions. If she loves you that will be enough to make her eternally happy but the lure of provisions is soon failing and divorce will soon follow. Make sure you are not just her clean-up crew; being the solution to all of her past bad decision. Make sure you are not just her private ATM, check out her credit ratings and bank accounts, if she is not forthcoming that is a red-flag. If her credit rating is bad or her checking account balance is near zero this is also a red-flag.

Men often make the mistake of desiring to be this 'damsel in destress' knight in shining armor. She will entice you to fulfill the role of her dragon slayer, but make no mistake you will not experience the storybook fable ending 'and they lived happily ever after'. You can't save her from herself, the dragon that seeks to destroy her is herself. She has been customized by the culture she was raised in. People can put up a front for a little while but they can't sustain it. If you are not diligent in your examination the true person will come to light in just a little while after you have married her.

Make sure she wants you and not just a man to take care of her problems. Then she will be incentivized to care for you. Make sure you are not looking for a slave, business partner, or bed warmer. A virtuous woman brings a wife to the table the modern woman brings only the results of her past mistakes.

Generally you won't find a good wife or a virtuous woman in a bar, club, or on social media and dating web-sites. Facebook, Tik-Tok, and Instagram are good social media sites to check to see if the one you are interested in has posted/revealed her true character. Warning!!! Social media opens a lot of doors that other men can and will approach your special one. Check to see if the one who has caught your eye frequents social media, if she does it is a red-flag because social media primarily promotes our godless society.

The man who is wise knows how to separate the sheep from the wolves. If you are looking for a pig you will find her waddling in the mud but not a lamb. If you are looking for a virtuous woman:

- Generally you won't find her the product of a single mother home
- Generally she won't be influenced by many girl friends
  - This is big red-flag with bells, girlfriends give bad advice for many different reasons: they advise from their emotions, from a misguided sense of worth, jealousy, the cult of the sisterhood, etc.
  - Girlfriends lead to girl-trips where nothing that benefits a marriage takes place.
- Generally she won't have a large body-count or boyfriends who have imprinted themselves upon her psyche.
- Generally she will be younger and not older
- Generally her FICA credit score will be above 650, anything less is a red-flag anything above 700 is a green-flag.
- Generally before you date her she will require that you meet her father, she will have some trusted male relative vet you for her.
- She will require marriage
- She will not be 'high maintenance'!
- She will not accept long courtships
- She will require that you be a mature Christian
- She will not have unrealistic expectations
  - She is not looking for Prince Charming to come and save her
- Generally up-front she will wait on you hand and foot
  - Sarah called Abraham 'lord'
- Generally she will be prudent
- Generally she will be frugal

- Generally she will be modest and not dress to attract the attention of men
- Above all she will be a student of the Bible

<u>Where do You Go to get a Virtuous Wife?</u>

The first step for a man to take in finding a virtuous wife is to fall in love with God's wisdom because God's wisdom will emanate from her.

The Virtuous Woman described in Proverbs is not an actual person, Proverb's context is the worth of Godly Wisdom therefore the virtuous woman of Proverbs describes the benefit of not possessing a woman but of possessing God's Wisdom. If you and your wife possess Godly Wisdom then the many benefits of Proverbs 31:10-31 will be manifested in your marriage.

Since Godly Wisdom is personified as the perfect wife then the perfect wife has the characteristics delineated in Proverbs 31:10-31.

Basically she will do you good all the days of her life. In the same way that Godly Wisdom benefits you in all the ways of your life a virtuous woman will benefit you in all the ways of your marriage; you will trust her, she will be a benefit to you, and you will praise her excellence.

Seek the woman who has Godly Wisdom for by definition she will exhibit the characteristics of a virtuous wife. I'm sure that you have retorted 'who can find such a woman?' You are not the first to ask Prov. 31:10 asks the same question 'An excellent wife, who can find her? For her worth is far above jewels.' The one who finds her prays to God incessantly for her and lives before God righteously.

<u>Something to Consider If You Can't Find a Wife</u>

> Though feminism is on the decline its foul scent still lingers on the modern woman.

Feminism is on the decline because the modern woman has begun to reject its lies.

Feminism has told the modern woman that it's all about her and that she should have it all. Well, having it all has proved to be too exhausting. The demands of the job, the demands of the kids, the demands of the husband, the demands of social relevance, the demands of self-fulfillment has proved to be too much work. Feminism is on the decline but Modernism is on the incline. Feminism has told the modern woman that she can have it all but the modern woman says she doesn't want it all. The modern woman rejects seeking fulfillment through the work-place but seeks to retain most of the other lies of feminism.[68] In particular they seek to retain the part that sprouts 'it's all about her'. Work has proved to be too demanding and since, in her mind, it's all about her comfort and convenience it makes sense to her to get married and live off the labor of her husband. When my children would come to me with their list of all the things they wanted me to get them my reply to them was always "there is never an end to the list of things you want!" and as such if you marry one of these modern women there will be no end to the things she wants you to do for her. Because after all the modern woman still holds onto the feminist mantra 'it's all about her'. Now this mantra is not found in a wife and has no place in a family because in the family dynamic 'it's all about the family'. Both husbands and wives, grandparents, uncles and aunts, sons and daughters, everybody is called on to make sacrifices for the betterment of the family. And the betterment of the family leads to the betterment of a godly society. Though feminism is on the decline its foul scent still lingers on the modern woman. Don't be fooled by the modern woman who tells you she wants to stay at home and be a wife, what she really means she is tired of working and is expecting you to take care of her and get her everything she wants. I know this is depressing and you are asking yourself, "then how do I know I have a winner?"

In Genesis chapter 24 the bible tells of a lovely event where Abraham tasks his servant Eliezer to find a wife for his only son Isaac. Why didn't Isaac find his own wife? Because Abraham had certain standards for his son's wife and didn't want him choosing from amongst what the world had to offer so Abraham would not leave it up to his son to choose a wife. The world is an evil place where good men are preyed upon by evil women. Abraham instructed his servant as to what type of woman he was to find for his son. There is something to be said for 'arranged marriages'. So what type of woman did Eliezer look for, the same type of woman you should look for.

- Gen. 24:16 The woman was very beautiful, a virgin; no man had ever slept with her. She went down to the spring, filled her jar and came up again. 17The servant hurried to meet her and said, "Please give me a little water from your jar." "Drink, my lord," she said, and quickly lowered the jar to her hands and gave him a drink. 19After she had given him a drink, she said, "I'll draw water for your camels too, until they have had enough to drink." 20So she quickly emptied her jar into the trough, ran back to the well to draw more water, and drew enough for all his camels. 21Without saying a word, the man watched her closely to learn whether or not the Lord had made his journey successful.

She was beautiful and she was a virgin, these were great attributes but these things were not what Abraham's servant looked for, 'he watched her closely as she gathered water for all those camels'. Now I don't know if you know it or not but the typical camel can drink 53 gallons of water in as little as three minutes. Abraham's servant just sat there and watched her draw all that water, but what do you think he saw? He saw the same things you should be looking for in a wife, someone not afraid of hard work and someone who has a servant's heart. After all you are required to serve your family and the wife you choose should not have the modern woman's attitude that 'it's all about her comforts and conveniences'. This is why the bible stresses not to become unequally yoked for if you do then you will have to bear not only your part of the family's burden but hers too. You will be left all alone pulling the family wagon while she has jumped into the wagon's cart with all her demands and become part of the load you have to pull.

So then you are divorced and have been freed to marry another or you have been so jaded by your previous marriage(s) that you have given up on finding a wife or you have never been married before and are looking for a wife. Resent options for the godly man have come to the fore. Because in our western culture virtuous women are as rare as hen's teeth some have suggested becoming passport Joes.

- The "Passport Joes" are men who have chosen to seek out foreign women, typically from Asian, South American or Eastern European countries, for relationships. They believe that western women have been influenced by cultural and societal pressures to behave untraditionally, and that by seeking non-western women they can find a more authentic, fulfilling, and harmonious relationship. This is seen as a way to avoid the "wickedness" of western women whose ideal husband is six-feet tall, has a six-pack, and earns at least six-figures as opposed to foreign women who are accustomed to male lead homes and therefore seek leadership capabilities in their potential husbands. Also these foreign women are attracted to the western man because they are not as demanding of relationships as the men in their own countries are.
- Passport Joes. don't bring the women they marry in foreign lands back home to America because the culture (western, modern-feminist) will contaminate them, turning them into the women that our society are currently having marriage problems with.
- Passport Joes. predominately but not exclusively search for more traditional women in Asian Countries where they find

the women have been raised to be wives but not necessarily Christian. Christian Passport Bros. should take to heart God's admonition not to be 'unequally yoked'.

  ○ 2 Corinthians 6:13 Be ye not unequally yoked together with unbelievers: for what fellowship hath righteousness with unrighteousness? and what communion hath light with darkness? 14 Do not be unequally yoked with unbelievers.

Some western men who can't exercise the Passport Joes option exercise the MGTOW option.

- MGTOW: The MGTOW ideology is centered on male separatism and strongly believes that feminism has corrupted society. All MGTOW groups share something in common; they are all misogynist and anti-feminist that believe feminism makes women dangerous to men. Therefore, male self-preservation calls for complete disengagement from women. They query 'Why would you sign a marriage contract that incentives women to break it?' The marriage contract is the most consequential contract you will sign without any understanding of the hole you have placed yourself in.[69]

The concept of MGTOW is applicable to Christians if their separation from females is so that they can focus their lives on serving the Lord.

- 1 Cor. 7:32 I would like you to be free from concern. An unmarried man is concerned about the Lord's affairs—how he can please the Lord. 33But a married man is concerned about the affairs of this world—how he can please his wife.) But if you can't remain celibate it is better that you marry.

- 1 Cor. 7:9 But if they cannot control themselves, they should marry, for it is better to marry than to burn with passion.

How Then Do You Find a Wife?

If Passport Joes. and MGTOW are not good options for you then how do you find a virtuous woman in the modern, western, feminist culture?

Make friends with the families of ladies from good homes who have been raised to be wives. You may possibly find them in home/nest building classes, definitely in bible studies. Beware of the woman in church, I know you think that if she attends a church she has a good relationship with God but not necessarily so.[70]

Genesis presents the prototype of all men in Adam and all women in Eve. So let's take a look at Eve's relationship with God and maybe we can learn something to become aware of as we search the churches to find a wife. In Genesis when Satan addresses Eve the bible describes it this way:

- Gen. 3:1 Now the serpent was more crafty than any of the wild animals the Lord God had made. He said to the woman, "Did God really say, 'You must not eat from any tree in the garden'?"

Did you catch that? No. Okay let's try it again and see if you can catch it.

- 2The woman said to the serpent, "We may eat fruit from the trees in the garden, 3but God did say, 'You must not eat fruit from the tree that is in the middle of the garden, and you must not touch it, or you will die.' "

Still didn't get it, I don't blame you. Satan is so subtle it's hard to see how such a little change can mean so much.

Okay then let's pull the covers off his deception. In the first chapter of Genesis God is creating everything and as Creator He is called God. But in the Second Chapter God recaps everything He has created but the emphasis is not on Him as creator but on Him as Lord.

- Gen. 2:1 Thus the heavens and the Earth were completed in all their vast array. 2By the seventh day God had finished the work he had been doing; so on the seventh day he rested from all his work. 3Then God blessed the seventh day and made it holy, because on it he rested from all the work of creating that he had done.

In my opinion the second chapter of Genesis should start at the fourth verse. Here God is now called Lord God.

- Gen. 2:4 This is the account of the heavens and the Earth when they were created, when the <u>Lord</u> God made the Earth and the heavens.

In the first chapter of Genesis God is presenting himself as the Creator and as such He has the right to allocate to Adam the right to rule over His creation but now in the second chapter of Genesis God is ruling over Adam by putting a single restriction on him.

- Gen. 2:16 And the Lord God commanded the man, "You are free to eat from any tree in the garden; 17but you must not eat from the tree of the knowledge of good and evil, for when you eat from it you will certainly die."

So God adds to His name Yahweh which changes from God (Elohim: one of strength and power, the infinite, all-powerful God who is the creator, sustainer, and supreme judge of the world) to Lord God; Yahweh is present, accessible, near to those who call on Him for deliverance (Psalm 107:13), forgiveness (Psalm 25:11) and guidance (Psalm 31:3).

Elohim speaks to what God is whereas Yahweh speaks to who God is, Yahweh/Jehovah is God's personal name. To use this name of God speaks of relationship, it is personal.

So when Satan address Eve in Gen. 3:1 the One who created Satan is not only his God but also his Lord but Satan doesn't consider the Lord God his Lord; that is One who is to be in relationship with, so when Satan address Eve he says to her "Did God really say, 'You must not eat from any tree in the garden'?" and she replied "We may eat fruit from the trees in the garden, 3but God did say, 'You must not eat fruit from the tree that is in the middle of the garden, and you must not touch it, or you will die.' "

This is a long way around to make a point but it is important to know when you consider church women for marriage. Like Eve many church women considers God (Elohim) her creator but not her Lord (Yahweh). In our example above Eve adopts the same attitude towards her Lord God that Satan does and refuses to address God as her Lord or Elohim as Yahweh.

I taught a young women's class in Church one week-day the topic being 'What is the role of woman in Church'. It got heated when I said that God doesn't approve of women being pastors because of 1 Tim. 2:12 'I do not let women teach[71] men or have authority over them. Let them listen quietly.' In anger one young lady rose up and shouted "Paul got it wrong!"

> There are many women who are religious but don't respect God as Lord.

There are many women who are religious but don't respect God as Lord. They will agree with scripture as long as scripture agrees with them. And if they are at heart feminist or modern you may have more trouble out of them than a woman who is not saved because a woman who is not saved has the chance of becoming saved and submissive by receiving the Word of God but a woman who has already rejected God's Word as her guide leaves you with nothing you can use to ever change her.

I officiate our New Members Orientation class where many applicants join our local church membership based on their 'Christian Experience' some with over 50 years of experience. I'm always amazed that when I ask them 'How do a person become saved' and they can't answer such a fundamental question. Now I'm not saying that they are not saved all I'm saying is that they can't explain to me how a person becomes saved. My amazement is as far as I take it because the only person I can affirm is saved is myself, judging other people's salvation is beyond my pay grade. I have not been given the responsibility to judge other's salvation but I would like to paraphrase Dr. J. Vernon McGee "I can't judge another's salvation but I am called to be a fruit inspector." You see a person who has a relationship with God produces 'good fruit'. So if the woman who has caught your eye professes to be a 'church goer' inspect her fruit.

This seems to be as good a place as any to ask you the question 'Are you saved?' If not then forget all that this book encourages because it is not written to you but is only applicable to those who are saved. If you are saved, explain to me just how were you saved? And if you don't know if you're really saved or not listen carefully:

- "Whoever has the Son has life; whoever does not have the Son of God does not have life" (1 John 5:12). Why is this? Because all have sinned (Rom. 3:23), both you and me and God is Just, He must punish sin. God is also Love therefore He sought a way whereby He doesn't have to punish you and me the sinners and still remain Just and punish your sins and mine. The way He found to do both; punish and Love the sinner is found in His Son Jesus the Christ. Jesus paid the penalty for the sins both you and me should have had to bear ourselves. Then He offered the payment He paid for our sins to us as a gift. He said you and me can't work for this gift, for if we could work for it, it would cease to be a gift. God's concern was that everybody would have access to Jesus' gift because He died for the sins of the whole world. But if God had put a price on it then some would not be able to pay the price so He made it free. All you have to do to receive God's gift of salvation is to place your trust in the fact that Jesus Christ died to pay the penalty for your sins. That's it, that is all you have to do, accept Jesus Christ's gift of salvation. But how do you know that you have accepted Jesus' gift of salvation, when you do then God's Holy Spirit takes up residence in you and begins a work of sanctification that changes who you were into becoming someone who resembles Jesus Christ.

ABOVE ALL LIVE RIGHTEOUSLY AND PRAY VIGOROUSLY, FOR A MAN WHO FINDS A GOOD WIFE IS BLESSED OF GOD. AMEN

There are so many wonderful things that happens to you when you place your trust in Jesus Christ but for now we are only concerned that you have placed your trust in the work that Jesus Christ did for you on His cross where He paid the penalty for your sins. If you trust in that and that alone then you are saved and have a relationship with God. And since you now have a relationship with God then pray to Him concerning your desire to acquire a wife because the man who finds a wife has been blessed of God. And since wives are very rare above all Pray, Pray, and

Pray some more as you live a righteous, godly, Christian life for the women who is virtuous will require you to be.

ABOVE ALL LIVE RIGHTEOUSLY AND PRAY VIGOROUSLY, FOR A MAN WHO FINDS A GOOD WIFE IS BLESSED OF GOD. AMEN

HAPPY HUNTING

[1] National Center for Family & Marriage Research

[2] wf-lawyers.com/divorce-statistics-and-facts

[3] one person's gain is equivalent to another's loss, so the net change in wealth or benefit is zero.

[4] An inflection point refers to a key event that changes the trajectory of some process or situation, in this case marriage.

[5] Helen Gurley Brown in 1962, the just-married copywriter penned Sex and the Single Girl, a fictional book about a swinging singleton who was leading this new kind of life. Not only did the book tell women they didn't need a man to be happy, but it also encouraged them to enjoy sex with whomever they damn well pleased — without guilt. (cosmopolitian.com)

[6] truthout.org/articles/sister-citizen-black-women-in-a-crooked-room

[7] Men control access to marriage women control access to sex.

[8] escaped punishment for something you should have been punished for

[9] mensdivorce.com/suicide-rates-high-divorced-men/

[10] Research into the views of US millennials found 12% of Hispanic women, 21% of African American women, 23% of Asian women and 26% of white women identify as a feminist.

[11] Women have an innate need not to recognize fault in themselves.

[12] crispandco.com/site/blog/family-law-blog/can-menopause-cause-relationship-breakdown

[13] gleneagles.com.sg/health-plus/article/common-signs-hormonal-imbalance-women

[14] hopkinsmedicine.org/health/conditions-and-diseases/introduction-to-menopause

[15] kellerlegalservices.com/blog/2023/02/13/why-fathers-should-always-protect-their-rights-with-a-paternity-test/

[16] Used to convey that the criticisms a person is aiming at someone else could equally well apply to themselves.

[17] headstuff.org/topical/marriage-and-feminism/

[18] Socially constructed expectations became traditions because they proved beneficial to society. After 50+ years of modern feminism its effect is the destruction of marriage and the de-evolution of womanhood.

[19] bible.org/seriespage/lesson-10-curse-and-covering-genesis-316-24

[20] A system of oppression in which men hold all the power and women are held captive to it.

[21] /india2020afeministnation.wordpress.com/2016/02/25/actual-feminism-vs-modern-feminism/

[22] Having unsuitable feminine qualities not possessing qualities befitting a man.

[23] observer.com/2016/05/five-ways-feminism-has-made-women-miserable

[24] This is essentially a way for a woman to say that she is living life to the fullest and achieving the full potential of enjoyment out of her life.

[25] The woman's brain is designed to be receptive to the imprinting of their sex partner (singular). Having multiple sex partners confuses the brain and causes a lack of bonding with one's husband, leading to higher divorce rates.

[26] www.lovetoknow.com/life/relationships/rates-divorce-adultery-infidelity

[27] Hook-up culture refers to a culture built on the approved practice of engaging in hook-ups, or sexual encounters between two or more individuals where it is understood that commitment, relationships, and emotional feelings are not expected outcomes.

[28] Ratchet means wretched and is used to describe someone or something as nasty and unappealing

The term is the urbanized version of "wretched." It is most often used to refer to a ghetto diva who is a gross looking and/or behaving person. The woman is also loud and obnoxious.

[29] A horse trainer who adopts a sympathetic view of the motives, needs, and desires of the horse, A person speaks to horses or has control over horses through whispering.

[30] Cortisol is an essential hormone that affects almost every organ and tissue in your body. It plays many important roles, including: Regulating your body's stress response. Helping control your body's use of fats, proteins and carbohydrates, or your metabolism.

[31] Become independent and live your best life, don't depend on no man because they can't be trusted, get your education so you can have something to fall back on when he divorces you and leaves you with all the children.

[32] An adult male living at home with his mother and/or siblings, who fulfills the emotional and intellectual needs of his mother at the expense of his own personal romantic and/or emotional development.

[33] foxnews.com/opinion/i-gen-z-men-my-generation-not-dating-why-should-we

[34] The Donor Dilemma: Black donor shortage hurts women looking for sperm. Analysis posted in October 2022 found Black men account for less than 2% of sperm donors at Cryobanks nationwide.

[35] I use the word 'spouse' because so few of us have 'wives'.

[36] Heart in Hebrew leb: inner man, mind, will and in Greek kardía; "the affective center of our being" and the capacity of moral preference

[37] Gen Alpha, term used to describe the generation of people born (or who will be born) between 2010 and 2025

[38] Women experience depression at roughly twice the rate of men. In 2021, it was estimated that 27.2 percent of women in the U.S. had some type of mental illness in the past year.

[39] The Greek words oikodomeo, "to build,". As used in the bible in the figurative sense, the promotion of growth in Christian character.

[40] Life Application Bible Commentary - Life Application Bible Commentary – Ephesians.

[41] www.supportivecareaba.com/statistics/average-attention-span

[42] kleinattorneys.com/exploring-the-latest-trends-in-us-divorce-data-2023-insights/

[43] Women always overvalue their worth and then after a while of living with you they undervalue your worth. This gives them the feeling that they should not have 'settled for you'.

[44] These programs offer testimonies of divorced women and their plight in the modern dating world.

[45] A man in the top one percent of earners has his choice of 99+% of all available women. That includes young, fit, friendly, beautiful, cooperative, submissive, and childless women.

[46] Marriage is a contract with the State, pair-bonding is a contract with God.

[47] Not all modern women are affected in the same way and to the same extent by the culture we live in today. These are just generalization you should be aware of.

[48] Child Well-Being in Single-Parent Families by the Annie E. Casey foundation updated on June 23, 2023

[49] Simp is when a male is overly submissive to a female and gains nothing from it.

[50] www.gotquestions.org/the-two-shall-become-one-flesh.html

[51] The wall means that females 35+ years of age begin losing their sexual power over men and face steep competition from younger, prettier women

[52] www.childstats.gov/americaschildren21/family2.asp#:

[53] Psychologists Galena K. Rhoades and Scott M. Stanley found that the study respondents who had sex with other people prior to marriage reported lower-quality unions compared to couples who slept just with each other. Multiple sex partners prior to marriage reduced marital quality for women, but not men. Along similar lines, sociologist Jay Teachman showed that premarital sex between future spouses didn't make divorce more likely, but sex with other people did.

[54] Vasopressin also plays a major role in defensive behaviors such as mate guarding... the physiological effects of vasopressin support physical mobilization and defensive aggression,...

[55] This is the idea behind Eph. 5:21 where you both are commanded to submit to each other.

[56] "Hypergamy." It is the female evolutionary instinct to prefer male sex partners of a higher socioeconomic class, wealth level, and/or resource potential.

[57] "After controlling for single motherhood, the difference between black and white crime rates disappeared." Progressive Policy Institute, 1990, quoted by David Blankenhorn, "Fatherless America: Confronting Our Most Urgent Social Problem," New York, Harper Perennial, 1996, p.31

[58] http://www.fathers.com/statistics-and-research/the-extent-of-fatherlessness/

[59] digitalcommons.liberty.edu/cgi/viewcontent.cgi?article=2244&context=honors

[60] Malachi 2:16 (NASB) "For I hate divorce," says the LORD, the God of Israel, "and him who covers his garment with wrong," says the LORD of hosts. "So take heed to your spirit, that you do not deal treacherously."

[61] Eccl. 5:4 When you make a vow to God, do not delay to fulfill it. He has no pleasure in fools; fulfill your vow. 5It is better not to make a vow than to make one and not fulfill it. 6Do not let your mouth lead you into sin. And do not protest to the temple messenger, "My vow was a mistake." Why should God be angry at what you say and destroy the work of your hands? 7Much dreaming and many words are meaningless. Therefore fear God.

[62] James 5:16b ...The effectual fervent prayer of a righteous man availeth much. (KJV)

[63] Whatever the issues we have with our spouses it is hard to imagine one more undesirable than unfaithfulness.

[64] Seek women who keep themselves as fit and beautiful as possible understanding that she is limited to her DNA.

[65] Research dating back decades finds that physically attractive people consistently receive preferential treatment, across a wide range of contexts, from pre-school to the job market.

[66] bibleask.org/who-is-the-strange-woman-that-is-mentioned-in-proverbs

[67] The young man is not an illustration of youth but of those who are not experienced with the ways of the ungodly world.

[68] Author Mona Charen says women are less happy today than they were before the second and third waves of feminism. She points to three ways the feminist movement made mistakes: endorsing the sexual revolution, denigrating family life, and insisting there are no differences between men and women.

[69] James Sexton renowned Divorce Attorney

[70] According to 'unsavedbeliever.net: How many regular churchgoing believers who might describe themselves as born again Christians are not saved? The consensus seems to be around 70 to 75%.

[71] The position of teacher (rabbi) intrinsically implied authority

Don't miss out!

Visit the website below and you can sign up to receive emails whenever Gordon Simmons publishes a new book. There's no charge and no obligation.

https://books2read.com/r/B-A-JOMCB-NCCTC

BOOKS 2 READ

Connecting independent readers to independent writers.

www.ingramcontent.com/pod-product-compliance
Lightning Source LLC
Chambersburg PA
CBHW051436130726
47987CB00005B/2077